N

a

Today

Martin Luther King and *THE TRUMPET OF CONSCIENCE* Today

Régine Michelle Jean-Charles

Dear Kelly,
I hope that this book
reminds you to always listen
for the trumpet of conscience that
centers justice! Blessings to you

ORBIS BOOKS

Maryknoll, New York 10545

Founded in 1970, Orbis Books endeavors to publish works that enlighten the mind, nourish the spirit, and challenge the conscience. The publishing arm of the Maryknoll Fathers and Brothers, Orbis seeks to explore the global dimensions of the Christian faith and mission, to invite dialogue with diverse cultures and religious traditions, and to serve the cause of reconciliation and peace. The books published reflect the views of their authors and do not represent the official position of the Maryknoll Society. To learn more about Orbis Books, please visit our website at www.orbisbooks.com.

Library of Congress Cataloging-in-Publication Data

Names: Jean-Charles, Régine Michelle, author.
Title: Martin Luther King and the trumpet of conscience today / Régine
     Michelle Jean-Charles.
Description: Maryknoll, New York : Orbis Books, [2021] | Includes bibliographical
     references and index. | Summary: "Examines Martin Luther King's series of speeches,
     The Trumpet of Conscience," as a point of departure for discussing contemporary
     issues facing us in the 21st century that demand a faith-based perspective with justice
     at the center"—Provided by publisher.
Identifiers: LCCN 2021011338 (print) | LCCN 2021011339 (ebook) | ISBN
     9781626984431 (trade paperback) | ISBN 9781608339068 (epub)
Subjects: LCSH: King, Martin Luther, Jr., 1929-1968. Lectures. Selections. | King, Martin
     Luther, Jr., 1929-1968—Influence. | King, Martin Luther, Jr., 1929-1968—Religion. |
     Social justice—United States. | Social justice—Religious aspects—Christianity. |
     Peace—Religious aspects—Christianity. | Racism—United States. | Church and social
     problems. | United States—Race relations. | United States—Social conditions.
Classification: LCC E185.97.K5 J425 2021 (print) | LCC E185.97.K5 (ebook)
     | DDC 323.092—dc23
LC record available at https://lccn.loc.gov/2021011338
LC ebook record available at https://lccn.loc.gov/2021011339

There is no such thing as a single-issue struggle because we don't live single-issue lives.

—Audre Lorde

for Ohene

Contents

Foreword

M. Shawn Copeland

Long before the devastating and malignant coronavirus squeezed the breath of life from millions of children, women, and men around our planet, long before the virus shredded the fabric of our national civic, cultural, and social life,[1] we peoples of the United States were gripped by what the Reverend Doctor Martin Luther King Jr. named the evils of racism, poverty and extreme materialism, and war and violence. King raised his voice to denounce these injustices and put his very body on the line in disciplined nonviolent civil disobedience. He responded to the demand of conscience to proclaim a new social vision grounded in faith in God to uphold the goodness of all humanity and to affirm the spiritual, cultural, and social (i.e., political, economic, technological) potential of our nation.

King was motivated by the "conviction that [all human beings] are made in the image of God, and that they are souls of infinite metaphysical value. "If we accept this as a profound moral fact," he asserted, "we cannot be content to see [them] hungry, to see [them] victimized with ill-health, when we have the means to help them."[2]

---

[1] To date, globally 3,351,157 human beings have died, and the US mortality figure nears 600,000.

[2] Martin Luther King Jr., *Where Do We Go from Here: Chaos or Community?* (New York: Harper and Row,1967), 180.

He was a global citizen who insisted that "disinherited people all over the world are bleeding to death from deep social and economic wounds."[3]

More than fifty years have passed since King's sonorous voice rang out scrutinizing the "signs of our times," urging us to repel the nightmare that those evils might spawn, calling us to enact God's justice and providence in an oppressive and anguished world. Yet too many of us have forgotten not only the sound of his voice but the piercing truths of his words. Some of us dismiss the causes for which he struggled, others tolerate the status quo in complacency, and still others anesthetize the radical substance of his vision and message.

In this work, my Boston College colleague Haitian American professor Régine Michelle Jean-Charles not only reassesses King and his vision and message as articulated in *The Trumpet of Conscience* but dispenses the sanitized "conventional domesticated image"[4] of King and recovers for today's readers the far-sighted, analytical, radical, complex man who thundered,

> The dispossessed of this nation—the poor, both white and Negro—live in a cruelly unjust society. They must organize a revolution against that injustice, not against the lives of the persons who are their fellow citizens, but against the structures through which the society is refusing to take means which had have been called for, and which are at hand, to lift the load of poverty."[5]

An insightful feminist literary scholar, a perceptive cultural critic, a brilliant classroom teacher, and a gifted stylist, Jean-Charles's critique reinterprets *Trumpet of Conscience*, five lectures that King

---

[3]Martin Luther King Jr., *The Trumpet of Conscience* (New York: Harper and Row, 1967), 53.

[4]Paul Street, "Remembering the Officially Deleted Dr. King," www.counterpunch.org, January 17, 2014.

[5]King, *Trumpet of Conscience*, 59–60.

presented over the Canadian Broadcasting Corporation (CBC) during November and December 1967, situating their major themes in our current roiling spiritual, cultural, and social context. Further, by differentiating between King's deployment of notions of equality, racial progress, and freedom, Jean-Charles clarifies our limp usage and anemic praxis as these are being tested both by the coronavirus pandemic and persistent hate crimes against Black, Latinx, Asian, and LGBTQI youth, women, and men. Through interrogating current manifestations of racism, sexual violence, and mass incarceration in our soul-sick society, Jean-Charles's critique does more; it re-symbolizes and reinvigorates the book's enduring purpose—to expose suffering and to urge humanity to answer the sound of conscience.

As a literary scholar and cultural critic, Jean-Charles's work advances critiques of dominant narratives—wherever, in whatever, and in whomever such narratives may be invested and mediated. Thus, she rigorously uncovers efforts to deify or idolize King and acknowledges both his improper behavior and the sexism that prevented him from forging alliances with Black women leaders and organizers.[6] Just as rigorously, without disregarding those failings and weaknesses, Jean-Charles refocuses attention on King's radical vision, his uncompromising work for social justice for all, and his personal commitment to love God. Given the precariousness of national and global living at every level—ecological and biological, psychological and personal, political and economic, cultural, religious, and intellectual—such refocusing is necessary.

Jean-Charles illumines "the pedagogical power"[7] of King's life, message, and vision to teach all of us about our various, necessary, and differentiated roles and tasks in repudiating the nation's interconnected evils of racism, poverty, war, and violence. By drawing our attention to the radical and intersectional character of these lectures, she helps us—especially *the young* among us—to discover

---

[6]See Michael Eric Dyson, *I May Not Get There with You: The True Martin Luther King Jr.* (New York: Free Press, 2001).

[7]Brandon M. Terry, "Fifty Years since MLK," *Boston Review* (Winter 2018): 11–30, quote at 12.

a voice that continues to speak for justice for all. By titling the final chapter of this volume "Making Justice Irresistible," Jean-Charles encourages us all—especially *the young* among us—to imagine "otherwise," to create "otherwise," to explore and engage mapmakers who chart justice "otherwise": the Movement for Black Lives (M4BL), "LoveWITHAccountability," and prison abolition.

In this exhilarating and engaging work, Régine Michelle Jean-Charles does a great service for our time, for our country, for a new generation of women and men of *all* races, cultural-ethnic groups, and nationalities. She retrieves the radical, compassionate, revolutionary vision and message of the Reverend Doctor Martin Luther King Jr. In her vital, indeed, urgent reinterpretation of his vision and message, Jean-Charles inspires us all to reclaim the meaning of being human in and with community/society, to act deliberately in joy and hope for justice. As King assured us, "The spirit is awake now; structures will follow, if we keep our ears open to the spirit."[8] How grateful we all ought to be that Régine Michelle Jean-Charles has been listening!

M. Shawn Copeland
Professor Emerita of Theology and African American Studies
Boston College
May 18, 2021

---

[8] King, *Trumpet of Conscience*, 51.

Acknowledgments

This book is first and foremost a product of God's grace. When Orbis approached me about expanding my short essay "Taking King out of the Box" into a book, I initially demurred. I was eventually persuaded largely due to the coaxing of my beloved, Ohene Asare, who wondered if this might be an "Isaiah moment" that I was called to. Throughout the writing, I have often had to pray, "Here I am, God. Is it I, God?" Having completed this book in the midst of a pandemic, I know more than ever that only the grace of God made it so. Many people have contributed to praying for me; thinking alongside me; being in conversation with me; listening to my thoughts about justice, Jesus, and gender; inspiring me; organizing with me; and believing in my ability to write for people beyond academia. I am so blessed to be surrounded by many different circles of genuine care.

I am grateful to my parents and sisters, whose unconditional love is a strong foundation upon which I still stand today. I am also blessed to have a true "family-in-love," the Asares, whose love, support, and scintillating conversations bring joy to my life. I am incredibly grateful for my church family at Pentecostal Tabernacle where the theme of "Biblical Justice" for 2021 was right on time. I am especially grateful for the social justice small group, the social justice prayer ministry, the high school Sunday school class, and the women's ministry where I have had the opportunity to share some of this work. I am so thankful for the women in the Shatter the Silence small group at Bethel AME Church for being co-laborers in the vineyard to end gender-based violence and hold the church accountable in the struggle. Thank you to Rev. Dr. Gloria White-Hammond and Dr. Tara-Brooke Watkins for your visionary leadership of this group! My sisters Maria Lawrence, Kia Martin, and Jody Rose prayed for me continually, encouraged me in my writing, and supported me in all things. I am convinced that their prayers opened my eyes to a more expansive vision that allowed me to see past this project as a "book about Martin Luther King." I am thankful for my fantastic writing group Nadève Ménard and Chantalle Verna for their friendship, insights, and accountability. I owe a debt of gratitude to the amazing ConstructHERS: Kimberly Dilday, Angela Pitter, Kristen Pope, Nicole Roberts-Jones, Essence Souffrant, and Oneeka Williams who are an endless source of inspiration and motivation. I will always cherish the gift of Soyica Colbert, who first encouraged me to read *The Trumpet of Conscience.* The A Long Walk Home family gave me much to consider and write about as I think about justice in the twenty-first century. Thank you especially to "my Tillet sisters," Salamishah and Scheherazade, for your vision, your leadership, and your care for the souls of Black women and girls. Special thanks to Mimi, for warning me that writing "trade books" is harder! Thank you to the "Council of Sisterfriends," who have made my pandemic mornings less monotonous and more enriching. Special thanks to my sister Tara Edelschick for gathering this group of phenomenal women. Thank you to Paul McMahon for shepharding this book and to Thomas Evans for the phenomenal cover art.

Throughout my time at Boston College, I have had many conversations, given lectures, and taught classes related to the topics that I explore in this book. I am grateful to the Black Faculty, Staff, and Administrators Association (BFSAA) for inviting me to deliver the keynote address for the annual Martin Luther King Jr. breakfast, effectively tilling the ground for planting the seed of these ideas. My wonderful colleagues in the African and African Diaspora Studies Program are an extraordinary bunch I am honored to be a part of: Amey-Victoria Adkins-Jones, Shawn Copeland, Allison Curseen, Rhonda Frederick, Kyrah Daniels, Jonathan Howard, Shawn McGuffey, Richard Paul, Martin Summers, and Anjali Vats.

I am grateful for every former and current BC student placed in my care, especially those in the "Where #BlackLivesMatter Meets #MeToo," Paris Noir 2019 summer abroad course, every cohort of Black Feminisms 101 since Fall 2009, and the Class of 2020 AADS senior seminar. One of my greatest joys at BC is belonging to a powerhouse community of women through the RISE Mentoring Program under the leadership of my dear friend Katie Dalton.

I have also had many opportunities to present excerpts from this work in faith and social justice circles in my town of Milton, for which I am deeply thankful. Thank you so much to all of the members of the Milton Anti-Racist Coalition, especially Farah Assiraj, Winston Daley, Beverly Denny, Vanessa Foster, Erin Hardy, Zakia Jarrett, and Scott Matthews. To my wonderful, beautiful, smart, special children Bediako Dessalines, Kwaku Toussaint, Farah-Adwoa Heureuse, and Afia Anacaona, may you develop a deep faith that always does justice and may you be the change you want to see in the world.

And finally, I am grateful beyond measure for my beloved, Ohene Kwaku Asare, to whom this book is dedicated and who saw me in it before I saw myself.

Introduction

"A Sick Society"

I keep telling you, this is a sick society.
—Rev. Dr. Martin Luther King Jr., 1963

This *is* a sick society. The same is true, if not even more so, in the twenty-first century. We are indeed a sick society. So very sick, in fact, that a global public health crisis forcing the entire world to pause could not pause the killing of Black people. It offered no respite from the reality of anti-Black racism and violence in the United States. Despite the fact that we had to rest from so many activities, including school, work, travel, leisure, entertainment, and church, the loss and devaluation of Black life manifest in racist violence continued. The pandemic could not pause police brutality, racist violence, nor racial terror meted out against Black and Brown people in this country. It could not stem the tide of white supremacy. Indeed racism has been a feature of American society since the arrival of the *Mayflower*, when multiple indigenous populations were wiped out to make way for the pilgrims, and then again in 1619 with the arrival of the first group of enslaved Africans on the shores of Virginia—racial injustice has been flagrantly persistent.

Just as the violence against Black people can be traced to slavery and colonization, the determination of Black resistance goes back just as far. From the advent of slavery onward, racism has been a feature of US democracy that the enslaved have resisted. The COVID-19 pandemic further amplified the problems of social inequity in our society as Black and Brown people were struck by the disease and subsequently died in disproportionate numbers. It quickly became clear that racial discrimination as well as the lack of access to health care multiplied the vulnerability of Black people during the pandemic, and the wealth gap exacerbated this vulnerability due to the disproportionate number of Black and Latinx people serving as essential workers. As one organizer expressed, "The coronavirus has been anything but a great equalizer. . . . It's been the great revealer, pulling the curtain back on the class divide and exposing how deeply unequal this country is."[1]

Indeed, the novel coronavirus has magnified divisions that have long existed in our society—whether it is the fact that Black and Brown people have disproportionately been infected with the virus or denied care, or, as the population of essential workers attests to, many Black and Brown people have had no choice but to go to work. The pandemic has magnified racial inequality in the United States— from who is able to social distance to who is disproportionately at greater risk of being vulnerable to the disease. As this global public health crisis unfolded, I wondered what our social justice warriors would think about this moment. I wondered how Harriet Tubman would lead raids at a time when people could not huddle together for warmth or comfort. What would Sojourner Truth say about the Black and Brown female essential workers leaving their families to care for others only to increase the potential risk of their own families when they return home? What would Martin Luther King say about the disparities in public health? Knowing that King was an advocate of the poor and the oppressed, I am confident that he would be appalled and dismayed by how health care has been one of the latest platforms for economic and racial injustice to take root.

---

[1] Abdi Latif Dahir, " 'Instead of Coronavirus, the Hunger Will Kill Us.' A Global Food Crisis Looms," *New York Times*, April 22, 2020.

Indeed, the plight of the poor was always foremost on his mind, and he was attentive to how class was operating in the lives of poor Black and Brown people.

Given King's enduring commitment to revealing how economic injustice plagues our society, how would he respond to how poverty has made people more vulnerable to COVID-19? How would he react to our current lack of access to health care causing more harm to people who are sick and poor, or to the racial wealth gap that has not improved since his death? How would King respond to the reality that 61 percent of Black people in the United States are still living in poverty or just above the poverty line?

In our sick society, the pandemic has also revealed what King referred to as the conjoined evils of racism, poverty, materialism, and militarism that shape our society with nefarious outcomes. It has unveiled how few people of conscience populate our government. It has emphasized that the vast majority of people in our society do not operate as people of conscience. It has set new terms for our collective need for transformation and justice in this world. In the words of one historian, "The pandemic will not create the social transformation we need, but it will set the terms for it."[2] If the terms are being set, then what should be clear to us is that our sick society still has an incredibly long way to go. With people suffering in this moment, would King say, as he did in *The Trumpet of Conscience*, that "disinherited people all over the world are bleeding to death from deep social and economic wounds"?[3] I suspect that he would— and that the persistence of these problems would grieve his heart.

In May 2020, three months after much of the northeastern United States was sheltering in place due to the COVID-19 pandemic, news about the pandemic gave way to a different illness. The fatal illness of racism reentered the spotlight after the video-recorded killing of

[2]Nikhil Pal Singh, "Reclaiming Populism: From the Dying World to the World We Want," *Boston Review*, April 29, 2020.

[3]Martin Luther King Jr., *The Trumpet of Conscience* (New York: Beacon Press, 2010), 55.

George Floyd was made public. In rapid succession, that same year saw a series of deaths and events that were met with widespread outrage. On March 13, Breonna Taylor was killed by Louisville police. On May 5—just seventy-four days after she was killed—Ahmaud Arbery was murdered by vigilantes while jogging in his Georgia neighborhood. May 16 also marked the ten-year anniversary of the violent death of Aiyana Stanley-Jones, a seven-year-old Black girl fatally shot in the head by a white police officer during a raid in Detroit. (Aiyana Stanley-Jones would have been seventeen years old and possibly graduating from high school in the class of 2020.) Tamir Rice, who was killed by police in Cleveland at the age of twelve, would have been eighteen this year, and possibly beginning college. On May 25, George Floyd was killed, or more precisely, he was suffocated to death by Minneapolis police officer Derek Chauvin, who put a knee on his neck for eight minutes and forty-six seconds while three other police officers stood and watched. Were it not for the bravery of a seventeen-year-old girl, Darnella Frazier, who captured the killing on camera, what happened to Floyd may have gone unnoticed. In that video, we hear Floyd's final words: "I can't breathe." He calls for his mother with his last breath. That sentence heard throughout the world—"I can't breathe"—is painfully familiar. "I can't breathe" haunts us because it recalls the death of Eric Garner, killed by a New York police officer in 2014. As a refrain, it is a reminder that we live in a sick society, in which Black people are gasping for breath, that Black people need to breathe. Then before summer 2020 had ended, another unarmed Black man was shot by police. This time, Jacob Blake was shot seven times in the back—*seven times in the back*—while his children watched from the car. Though Blake continues to live, he remains paralyzed from the waist down. By the end of the summer of 2020, it became commonplace to observe that the United States was facing two pandemics—COVID-19 and anti-Black racism.

I wonder how Martin Luther King would have reacted to these deaths. What would he have to say about Breonna Taylor, Ahmaud

Arbery, or George Floyd? Having witnessed the deaths of Black girls like Carole Robertson, Cynthia Wesley, Addie May Collins, and Denise McNair who died as a result of the Ku Klux Klan bombing of a Birmingham church, what would he say about seven-year-old Aiyana Stanley-Jones killed by police in Detroit? Would King, who once said that "for the 35 million poor people in America—not to mention, just yet, the poor in other nations—there is a kind of strangulation in the air,"[4] associate the sentence "I can't breathe" with the strangulation in the air that is systemic injustice? Would he invoke the sacred promise of breath and its biblical significance? How would Martin Luther King respond to the torturous refrain of "I can't breathe"? Would he, like William Barber, return to the etymology of the word "breath" and its *pneuma*, which references the wind and reminds us that breath is holy? Would he, like the august theologian M. Shawn Copeland, offer a reflection of that breath to guide us in a meditation rooted in *ruah*, asking how the Spirit would respond to Black deaths? As Copeland writes,

> Pentecost came early this year: divine *ruah* broke through the walls of our here-and-now, interrupting racial oppression, instigating hope and action for change. In Hebrew, the word *ruah* denotes spirit, breath, and wind, and it is almost always connected with the life-giving attribute of God. Spirit-*ruah*— paradoxical, elusive, uncontrollable, absolutely free, repeatedly entering into human history—inspires, exhorts, reproves, prompts, animates, empowers, and sustains human persons in our active imaginative engagement with one another, and with the transcendent Triune God. The breath of Spirit-*ruah* rushes through our land. Can we hear it crying out in a dying man's words—"I can't breathe"? Can we feel the energy of Spirit-*ruah* rousing hundreds of thousands of people to protest the deaths of George Floyd and of so many others suffocated by

---

[4]King, *Trumpet of Conscience*, 56–57.

white racist supremacy? Can we allow ourselves to be moved
by the power of Spirit-*ruah* to understand what it would mean
to be *able* to breathe freely in America?[5]

Or, would King, like Reverend Kaji Dousa of Park Avenue Christian Church in New York City, be overcome with a holy rage that
drives her into the streets to lead protests? What would King say
about Breonna Taylor, who, relative to the men killed at the beginning of 2020, has inspired far less outcry and action? Breonna lay
asleep in her bed when police burst through the door and shot her
dead. Would King take to social media as so many have and demand
justice day after day, week after week, while her killers remain at
large? Would he use the pulpit to protest like the Reverend Otis
Moss, whose sermon "Between the Cross and the Lynching Tree"
revisits the words of the venerated theologian James Cone to lament
and prophesy new hope for this generation?

The similarity between the theologies of James Cone and Martin
Luther King has been noted by many previous scholars. They both
espoused similar views of racism, economic injustice, and the necessity for the person of faith to address these issues. Cone, however, has
clearly placed the burden of reconciliation squarely on the shoulders
of those with the most power and ability to change the system. "The
ever-present violence of white supremacy—psychic, physical and
spiritual—in the black community should be the chief concern of
white Americans. Reconciliation is a white responsibility."[6] Cone
has also gone to great lengths to decry the pervasiveness of white
supremacy in our society, especially in churches and in theology.

Would King decry the injustice of incarcerated people held
captive in prisons? What would he say about the prison industrial

---

[5]M. Shawn Copeland, "Breath & Fire: The Spirit Moves Us toward Racial
Justice," *Commonweal*, July 8, 2020.

[6]James Cone, *Said I Wasn't Gonna Tell Nobody: The Making of a Black Theologian* (Maryknoll, NY: Orbis Books, 2018), 47.

complex, given his commitment to the gospel and a Christ who came to set the captives free? Would he be disgusted that the US prison population has swelled to more than 2.1 million people and morphed into a system that the scholar Michelle Alexander aptly describes as the "new Jim Crow"? Would he look at mass incarceration and see it for what it is, a crisis that is afflicting the poor and vulnerable in disproportionate numbers?

Would the last words of George Floyd grab hold of King and jolt him out of a pandemic sleep into a new nightmare of American racism?

> *I can't breathe.*
> *I can't breathe.*
> *I can't breathe.*

It is a haunting refrain that strikes us even harder now in 2020 as we live through the realities of a pernicious pandemic—a respiratory virus that literally takes breath away from Black and Brown people in alarming numbers. Just as COVID-19 sucks life away from the lungs of those who are stricken by it, racism is both the air that we breathe and the system that takes our breath away.

Sadly, and as many of us are painfully aware, the tragic loss of and disregard for Black lives is not unique to the twenty-first century. It is far from new. It is why King fought, and preached, and protested, and taught the way he did decades ago. It is far from new, because we have been here before. Most Black and Brown people in the United States are not surprised when lives are senselessly taken, or when Black lives seem not to matter to people outside of ourselves. We have been in a space of mourning over the tragic loss of life of our Black brothers and sisters for most of the twenty-first century. Not only since 2013 when the hashtag #BlackLivesMatter was first used after the acquittal of George Zimmerman, the man who killed seventeen-year-old Trayvon Martin, or again after the death of Michael Brown in 2014, or when #SayHerName was set in motion by the death of Rekia Boyd, and, in fact, any time police officers kill Black people and are found not guilty by juries—not only in the twenty-first century.

As King knew far too well in the 1950s and 1960s during the civil rights movement, Black people fought for their right to be human and were faced with ongoing terror. The realities of lynching, being brutalized and beaten by the police, inflictions of state and vigilante violence were quotidian realities not unique to the mid-twentieth century. Racial terror has been a feature of life in the United States for more than four excruciating centuries. The fact is that it has been occurring since 1619 when the first group of Africans were brought to this country and enslaved. We have been here before. The protests are familiar, the groundswell is familiar, the chanting refrain of "Black lives matter" is familiar. And yet, it *feels* different now. We have been here before, but not like this . . . because we are in a pandemic. We are in a global public health crisis because of which the entire world is forced to pause. Yet the racial terror that Black people are subject to in the United States is not on pause, as these deaths remind us. It persists mercilessly and without impunity.

> *I can't breathe.*
> *I can't breathe.*
> *I can't breathe.*

Gasping for air we cry, we post on social media, we call our representatives, we pray and protest, we work for change, we attempt to explain why to our children when we have no answers ourselves. We look for ways to engage in direct action. We support antiracist organizations and raise bail funds. We provide booklists for our white friends and neighbors; we hope that they actually read the books and their children are raised differently so that our children will be safer. We accept speaking engagements, we write op-eds to contextualize rebellion, we go on television to add context to the pain, to explain, and to perform. We shed tears in the car, or in any quiet time we have to ourselves. We are not okay. We cry in anguish

. . . all without pausing for breath. We beg God to have mercy on us and make it all stop. We channel our rage and our heartbreak into activism. We preach sermons, lead protests, write columns, write to our public officials, teach our children, and encourage people to vote. We try not to lose hope. These are the forms of activism that have become commonplace in the twenty-first century. Protesters are still met with violence by police. Tear gas is still sprayed on innocent faces. People are still rounded up and put in jail for protesting.

> *I can't breathe.*
> *I can't breathe.*
> *I can't breathe.*

Today just as before, we can say that "this is a sick society." As the quotation that begins this book makes clear, Rev. Dr. Martin Luther King did not mince words in describing the state of the nation. He spoke the language of lament as frequently and as poignantly as he spoke the language of exhortation. He expressed sorrow as much as he prophesied. While we choose to focus on his prophetic anointing and how he dreamed of a more just future, we would do well to explore how the moral mission of his work operated according to a logic of calling things out. In fact, lament is essential to our struggle for social justice. Without lament, we cannot fully express the pain and the suffering to which we are subject. Without lament, we cannot readjust our vision to see the hope on the horizon. Without lament, we cannot feel our feelings and not to feel those feelings is to deny our humanity as we pursue change.

Our critique of "call-out" and "cancel culture" in the twenty-first century has become a way to chide young people for not being as peace-loving as their predecessors like King. I agree that people, as human beings, are not meant to be cancelled. But as a college professor, I have listened to my students explain that "calling out" and "cancelling" is one of the only ways to assert power—however tenuously—for those who do not have enough. In fact, the determination to admonish this generation is so pervasive that even King's own children have been challenged for what others erroneously perceive as misunderstanding his vision. But in fact, "calling out" people was as important a part of King's work as "calling in." He called out the wealthy; he called out white people; he called out the government; he called out Christians; he called out the white moderate; he called out his Black brothers and sisters. So when we accuse young people of deploying call-out culture for deplorable ends, we are overlooking a history and a tradition.

Even while the virus kills Black people at an unrelenting rate, the other sources of death in our lives tragically prevail. Furthermore, when we recall that King also referenced the "very legitimate anger" against racial injustice, we know that our anger is not the problem.[7] Anger was not a foreign emotion to King. More importantly, anger was not an emotion that Jesus shied from. What would King say to this generation today? What would he say to the young people like my students who are hungry for real change, frustrated by the lack of progress, and disheartened by how long this struggle has been waged? How would King react to the continued devaluation of Black life and the persistent threats against our humanity and dignity today?

To be clear, this is not a book *about* Rev. Dr. Martin Luther King. Rather, it is a reflection on what we can learn when we take the insights of King's last set of lectures and apply that wisdom to contemporary social justice issues. What happens when we listen to *The Trumpet of Conscience* and discern how it resonates today? In other words, I am interested in thinking about what would you—as an activist, a student, a believer, a parent, a feminist—say today if your conscience left you no other choice? Would you speak out against the global refugee crisis? Would you decry the injustice embedded in the Palestine-Israel conflict? Would you condemn the ravages of climate change? Would you stand unequivocally with rape survivors all over the world? This book takes these questions seriously, using *The Trumpet of Conscience*—in my view one of the

---

[7]King, *Trumpet of Conscience*, 60.

woefully understudied works of Dr. King—as a point of departure. The book asks you to focus on the radical parts of his vision and seeks to apply them to our contemporary moment. It recognizes and mulls over comments like the one King made on April 4, 1967, in a speech at Riverside Church in Manhattan, in which he said, "Freedom is never voluntarily given by the oppressor, it must be demanded by the oppressed." This speech, in which King spoke candidly, and against the advice of others, about the Israel-Palestine conflict, was a moment that helps to capture his radical vision. It gives us a glimpse into the fullness of his vision and helps us to imagine how he would respond to social justice issues unfolding in the twenty-first century. Like Brandon Terry and Tommie Shelby, I concur that in our remembrance of King, "It is imperative that we consider what his thought still has to teach us about how to build a more just and peaceful world."[8]

What do we learn when we wrestle with the parts of King's vision that make us uncomfortable, based on readings of *The Trumpet of Conscience*? How do the social justice issues we are facing today benefit when we apply King's vision? Alternatively described as "King's Call to Peace," these lectures from 1967 are a bold critique of what he calls the triple American evils of racism, materialism, and militarism. Throughout, he lambasts the evils of racism, the scourge of poverty, the snare of capitalism, and the horrors of war. This book asks the questions: What does King's call to peace look like today? What does peace mean to us today? How might we take some of the lessons in *The Trumpet of Conscience* written over fifty years ago and apply those to our current visions for racial justice, gender justice, and socioeconomic inequalities? Throughout I explore and offer a Black feminist and faith-based understanding of pressing social justice issues, all the while asking questions similar to the ones King posed in his speeches.

A powerful example from another one of King's speeches that I

---

[8]Brandon Terry and Tommie Shelby, *To Shape a New World: Essays on the Political Philosophy of Martin Luther King, Jr.* (Cambridge, MA: Harvard University Press, 2020), 2.

return to throughout this book comes from "I've Been to the Mountain-top." This speech was given in support of striking sanitation workers in Tennessee, and in it King retells the story of the "Good Samaritan" and ends by suggesting that those who refused to stop for the wounded man on the road ask, "If I stop to help this man what will happen to me?" However, the Good Samaritan reverses the question and asks, "If I do not stop to help this man, what will happen to him?" Today, people committed to social justice must ask these kinds of questions: "If I do not stop to help families separated at the border, what will happen to them?"; "If I do not stop to help Syrian refugees, what will happen to them?"; "If I do not stop to help those suffering as a result of income inequality, what will happen to them?"; "If I do not stop to help survivors of rape and sexual abuse, what will happen to them?"; and "If I do not stop to help #BlackLivesMatter activists, what will happen to them?" As Vincent Harding points out in *An Inconvenient Hero*, the questions that animated King's conscience were "Who is my neighbor" and "What does love demand?"[9] What interests me about King's framing of the Samaritan story is that it extends far beyond our current understanding of the term "ally" whereby the goal is to put love and justice at the center of how we interact with people who are marginalized, so that we ask: How do we create more justice? How do we imagine "allyship" differently?

Of the era of the 1960s, King said, "These are revolutionary times; all over the globe men are revolting against old systems of exploitation and oppression."[10] "Revolutionary times" might also be a way to describe how the next decade of the twenty-first century is unfolding. When we take into consideration the Arab Spring of the 2010s, the rise of the Black Lives Matter movement, and the global reckoning with sexual assault that #MeToo inspired, we are in a moment of multivaried resistance to systems of exploitation and oppression. When King made this point in "Conscience and the

---

[9]Vincent Harding, *Martin Luther King: The Inconvenient Hero*, rev. ed. (Maryknoll, NY: Orbis Books, 2013), 13.

[10]King, *Trumpet of Conscience*, 34.

Vietnam War," he was also undoubtedly reflecting on the wave of decolonial resistance that was sweeping across the African continent. King spurned the machinations of oppression and exploitation that were manifesting throughout the world and affecting marginalized people. Taking his position against the violent inhumanity of colonialism, racism, and war as his guide, King spoke out against Vietnam, because he felt obliged by conscience to do so. Heeding the call to peace means taking a similar view of twenty-first-century resistance struggles. It also means moving beyond knowing and articulating the vision to putting the words into action.

The chapters that follow focus on three social justice issues and movements from a perspective that is informed by King's call to peace. Throughout I bring my insights as a Black feminist scholar, a professor, a follower of Jesus Christ, a daughter of immigrants, an activist, and a mother committed to justice, joy, and advocacy. The lectures that make up *The Trumpet of Conscience* fascinate me because the topic of the speeches was left entirely up to King. He was given no guidelines—only the space and the freedom to speak his mind about any subject at all. In other words, he was free to choose whatever he wanted to talk about, and his choice of these topics then might reveal what was closest to his heart. *Martin Luther King and* The Trumpet of Conscience *Today* offers a unique window into his radical vision for the United States and for the world. We have much to learn from those lectures, and my hope is that by revisiting their insights we can imagine and create a more just future for the world.

Beyond the Dream

*It is easier to build monuments than to build a better
world.*

—Carl Wendell Hines Jr.

"A DEAD MAN'S DREAM"

Written only five years after the assassination of Martin Luther
King Jr., Carl Wendell Hines's poem "A Dead Man's Dream" is
prophetic and haunting. At the time of its writing, this poem issued
a cautionary tale. Read today, the poem convicts; it foretells exactly
how the public will interact with King's memory for generations
to come. It rightly accuses us today for not being more faithful to
the original vision and is emblematic of how easily and frequently
memorialization of Dr. King falls woefully short:

> Now that he is safely dead,
> Let us praise him.
> Build monuments to his glory.
> Sing Hosannas to his name.
> Dead men make such convenient heroes.
> For they cannot rise to challenge the images
> That we might fashion from their lives.

It is easier to build monuments
Than to build a better world.
So now that he is safely dead,
We, with eased consciences will
Teach our children that he was a great man,
Knowing that the cause for which he
Lived is still a cause
And the dream for which he died is still a dream.
A dead man's dream.

The poem eloquently expresses what happens when King's words and the memory overshadow the meanings and actions behind the words. While we are dazzled by the power of King's prose and the tenor of his speeches, we need to dig deeper into the content. It evokes the classic dichotomy between theory and praxis. In theory, we want to honor the man, but in praxis, we only honor the memory. "A Dead Man's Dream" condemns, and at times even accuses. How am I, the reader, guilty of the behavior the poet describes? By beginning with "now that he is safely dead," Hines immediately indicts us, suggesting that we prefer the dead King to the living one. "Safely dead." Hines, here, seemingly acknowledges the widespread public reaction to a radical King. Considering that, when Martin Luther King died, he was far from the height of his popularity, we know now that these words are true. When we "teach our children that he was a great man, knowing that the cause is still a cause," we fail to go beyond trite representations of King into the substance of his vision, teaching, and philosophy.

"A Dead Man's Dream" also acknowledges King's disclosure made in one of his final speeches: "Not long after talking about that dream I started seeing it turn into a nightmare."[1] The dream became a nightmare because it morphed into the main message, the only message. That King's dream so quickly mutated into a

---

[1] King, *Trumpet of Conscience,* 76.

nightmare—by his own admission, no less—is a revelation that should give us pause any time we invoke "I Have a Dream." The poem articulates a difficult truth that regularly gnaws away at my mind. We have become so obsessed with *the idea of the dream* that we have forgotten its actual overall vision. We have forgotten what motivated the dream. The dream is but a moment. It is a snapshot of the broader, more capacious vision and the longer goal for justice. The struggle for Black freedom in the United States and in King's lifetime centers on liberation and action. This is why Vincent Harding calls King a "hero who insists on living for the broken and exploited."[2]

Hines's somber poem "A Dead Man's Dream" resonates with me for various reasons. It encapsulates some of my own reservations about approaching a topic as vast and as ubiquitous as the legacy of Rev. Dr. Martin Luther King Jr. As a Black feminist literary scholar and cultural critic, I have grown both wary and weary of MLK Day celebrations to the extent that, every auspicious January, that day fills me with frustration. Even the use of abbreviation to refer to the Reverend Dr. Martin Luther King reminds me of our society's proclivity for shorthand. We use those letters as a quick, facile way of referring to the man and the myth. The easy, rapid references mirror the quick and thoughtless celebrations that we see in January of every year as this country, the United States, invokes MLK. For example, there are the "days of service." Last year, at my children's elementary school in a Massachusetts suburb, the students engaged in activities like making care packages for the police or donating items to an animal shelter. I found these choices mind-boggling. What does an animal shelter have to do with Martin Luther King? How do these activities for service reflect the racial and economic justice for which he fought? In what way do they attack the values of militarism, materialism, and racism still ensnaring the country? Does creating care packages for the police do anything to address

---

[2]Harding, *Martin Luther King*, 22.

the widespread problem of police brutality, which at its core is a manifestation of racial injustice?

King's Philosophy

Even the term *racial injustice* does not seem like an adequate descriptor these days. I get frustrated by the choice of *racial* rather than *racist* because in my view the former is a way to mask the latter. We are not comfortable calling people, institutions, or policies *racist*. I have seen this happen repeatedly in my town and at the university where I work. There is a fear of speaking racism even as it runs rampant in our schools, government, and institutions—injustice with racism at its root. In a society made up of many who refuse to acknowledge that racism is one of the most pervasive and persistent features of American culture, expressions that use *racial* rather than *racist* shrink back from that harsh reality. To combat racism, we must name it. The tendency to address racial injustice in such perfunctory ways is rampant throughout the United States. In fact, this is why scholars including Ibram X. Kendi have led the charge in driving us away from the language of racist and racism to embracing the term *antiracist*, because the latter shifts our attention to the active component necessary to fight racism. A term like *antiracism* does more to advance the struggles that King espoused because it is focused on action. It asks us to be active in the movement toward justice. It emphasizes movement and is inherently dynamic.

We can't know for sure how King would respond to the term *antiracist* today, but for clues we can examine the philosophy behind his teachings. Clearly, he would embrace the emphasis on action. Reverend King often worked unrelentingly to shift our attention to the need for action as well as to the imagination. King also expressed concern about how progress was being defined during the civil rights movement in ways that he deemed were reductive.

The lectures that form *The Trumpet of Conscience* differentiate between equality, racial progress, and freedom. Freedom, or liberation, goes far beyond ending segregation. Those who are convinced that we have come so far since his death are more concerned with racial progress narrowly defined than with Black freedom broadly defined. What does our freedom require? Freedom is decidedly different from civil rights, because it is not about accruing a set of policies. It is about the total liberation of people from the multiple oppressions that ensnare and limit. Justice is exactly what freedom should look like, and this series of lectures, given fewer than six months prior to King's death, point to his future vision and direct us toward freedom as the ultimate goal. At the very least, *The Trumpet of Conscience* asks that we take freedom seriously by imagining it and working toward it.

Celebrating King

From my own 1980s childhood in the affluent and predominately white suburb of Wellesley, Massachusetts, I have few memories of any King speeches, other than the one he made during the March on Washington. I recall that we would listen to or recite the "I Have a Dream" speech, but we never learned about any of his other speeches, writings, or teachings. We did not know about "Letter from a Birmingham Jail," in which he explains to fellow clergy, "I am in Birmingham because injustice is here," and claims that we must be proximate to injustice in order to combat it. At the Catholic elementary school I attended, we rarely discussed injustice or justice. In fact, my understanding of Jesus as a justice warrior came from my home, not from my school. At school, I only learned about Martin Luther King during that one day in January. My school was also one in which race or racism was never mentioned although both clung perniciously to our school culture from curriculum to social behaviors. For most of my elementary school years I was the only Black child in class, and when the lesson would turn to slavery, all of my classmates would look at me, reminding me of my difference.

Fortunately, my lessons about King and Black history did not depend solely on my formal education. I am the youngest child of Haitian immigrant parents, who took tremendous pride in their Black identity, taught their children about African American history, and encouraged us to learn more about our culture. By the time I was born, my parents felt more freedom and security in their parenting, social status, and reality of their citizenship, and were thus able to loosen their grip on parenting. The history of slavery that I was most familiar with inhabited my mind thanks to the many informal lessons about the Haitian Revolution that I had been fed from a young age. As member of the speech team in middle school, I performed works rooted in African American history, like Margaret Walker's poem about Harriet Tubman, in which she describes how Black Mother Moses worked to free other enslaved people—even before her story was screened on prime time. One of the books that my parents gave me before they moved back to their native country, Haiti, was the complete essays and speeches of Martin Luther King Jr. In high school, the instruction was slightly more attentive. There was one year when Cornel West came to speak for the annual celebration. His voice rising and falling in a cadence reminiscent of King, West preached to the predominately white audience of my elite prep school. The Black students were elated. We saw ourselves in his bushy Afro and heard ourselves in his strident words. We hoped that, with his help, our predominately white school would do more to address and combat racism. In the end, his appearance was symbolic rather than evidence of more meaningful social change.

Today, in our robustly digital world, examples of easy and quick celebrations of MLK abound on the internet. The Google image of King surrounded by people of different races remains on screen for twenty-four hours, just enough for people to remember this great hero who dreamed of a color-blind society. Schools enact days of service in a fleeting nod toward justice that is nowhere present throughout the remainder of the school year. Corporations launch a day of service, which is really just that—only a day. "A Dead Man's Dream" names and contradicts these practices, refusing to capitu-late to an easy and simplistic view of Martin Luther King. Many of these activities of remembrance are done out of a reverence for tradition that is ultimately thoughtless. As a Black feminist scholar,

I understand tradition as something to be critiqued and interrogated. Tradition for tradition's sake is empty.[3] Our call is to disrupt the traditions that do not serve us.

My frustration with the days of remembrance and what I deem vacuous celebrations extends from my view that the King we celebrate lacks nuance. He is flat and without substance. We are elevating the person to being merely a symbolic icon—a deified version of a man that lacks humanity. It is not faithful to who he actually was nor what he ultimately stood for. It is not born from a longing to see King's vision actually implemented but rather to show how much progress has been made. It is far too comfortable, because Martin Luther King was actually not interested in comfort at all. One of my pastors used to always tell us that God is not concerned with our comfort; God cares about our character. Her point is powerful because we live in a society in which a desire for comfort structures so much of our lives.

I am often frustrated that how we celebrate Martin Luther King now seems to have so little to do with what he actually said and what he actually did, especially toward the end of his life when he became increasingly radical. I am not the first to make this argument. As Cornel West reminds us in the introduction to *The Radical King*, the sanitized version of the preacher who has become a national hero falls short, because it obscures his radical vision. Rather, it is a convenient and comfortable snapshot of a more complicated picture that we prefer not to deal with. And as a literary scholar and cultural critic, I critique dominant narratives, interrogating the construction of myths, deconstructing images, and asking why some voices resound so much more loudly than others. Why, within so many different communities, are some people—usually men—elevated and venerated, while women's voices are marginalized, ignored,

---

[3]Mary Helen Washington notes, "Tradition. Now there's a word that nags the feminist critic. A word that has so often been used to misrepresent women." Quoted from Angelyn Mitchell, ed., *Within the Circle: An Anthology of African American Literary Criticism from the Harlem Renaissance to the Present* (Durham, NC: Duke University Press, 1994), 444.

elided, or forgotten? For those who care about justice and gender in
the context of Black freedom movements, Martin Luther King is a
towering figure whose ubiquity obscures the likes of others—both
men and women, but perhaps especially women—who toiled for
justice alongside him. This is why, for me, thinking about Martin
Luther King also means thinking about Ella Baker (1903–1986),
Fannie Lou Hamer (1917–1977), and Prathia Hall (1940–2002).[4]
It also means thinking about why and how we celebrate Martin
Luther King, and attempting to unravel the meanings behind our
celebrations and commemorations, as well as trying not to replicate
the dominant King narrative. It means not just doing what is quick
and easy; it means moving beyond the shorthand.

The mainstream determination to narrowly focus on King's
color-blind vision and his "I Have a Dream" speech is even more
perplexing when we consider how often he explicitly decried the
problem of systematized, institutionalized racism and the need to
dismantle it in all of his writings. *The Trumpet of Conscience* is no
exception. Embracing the metaphor of shadows and darkness he
so often deployed, King quotes Victor Hugo, saying that "we must
critique the one who created the darkness." In order to illuminate
the darkness and those who created it, we must tear down and
re-create the entire system. The radical nature of this perspective
unmistakable. It was King who said that "there must be more than a
statement to the larger society; there must be a force that interrupts
its functioning at some key point."[5] He also notes that "the policy
makers of the white society have caused the darkness: they created
discrimination; they created slums; they perpetuate unemployment,
ignorance, and poverty. It is incontestable and deplorable that Negroes have committed crimes, but they are derivative crimes. They
are born of the greater crimes of white society."[6] *The Trumpet of*

---

[4]See Barbara Ransby, *Ella Baker and the Black Freedom Movement: A Radical
Democratic Vision* (Chapel Hill: University of North Carolina Press, 2005).

[5]King, *Trumpet of Conscience*, 76.

[6]Martin Luther King Jr., "The Crisis in America's Cities," © 1967 Martin Luther

Conscience illuminates King's view of a sick society with a deeply rooted problem that requires systemic overhaul to create lasting change. King is absolutely correct in his assessment—"Of course, by now it is obvious that new laws are not enough"—because while policy initiatives and laws are important, they are not all that it takes to transform the world.[7]

RECALLING KING

Moving beyond the shorthand also calls us to remember that King was flawed.[8] He was human and therefore imperfect. As a Black feminist, those imperfections gnaw at my intellect and my spirit. His infidelity was exposed after his death and was the subject of many salacious articles. Even Michael Eric Dyson notes, "I could not conscientiously write a book about [King] without acknowledging [his] promiscuity."[9] When the FBI released its archives of many years of data that were gathered to discredit King, the ethical myopia of making him into an angelic figure was revealed. Even more perniciously, in an article for a conservative magazine, Martin Luther King biographer David Garrow alleges that King looked on and did not prevent a rape from taking place.[10] The accusations are indeed disturbing and damning. The different reactions to them suggest that the camps at either extreme—those wishing to demonize or deify King—have much at stake. This latest debate surrounding the King legacy exemplifies the problem of how rigid we have become

---

King Jr., excerpted in *The Atlantic*'s special coverage of Martin Luther King Jr.'s legacy, March 31, 2018.

[7]King, *Trumpet of Conscience*, 56.

[8]Michael Eric Dyson, *I May Not Get There with You: The True Martin Luther King Jr.* (New York: Free Press, 2001). Dyson states, "He was a man who was deeply human, deeply flawed, and yet truly amazing" (xv).

[9]Dyson, *I May Not Get There with You,* xi.

[10]David J. Garrow, "The Troubling Legacy of Martin Luther King," Standpoint, June 2019, https://www.davidgarrow.com/wp-content/uploads/2019/05/DJGStandpoint2019.pdf.

in remembering him. Even his good friend Ralph Abernathy wrote a book, *The Walls Came Tumbling Down*, in which he countered the "childish deification" of King to reveal some of his most pernicious flaws, including a penchant for extramarital affairs.[11]

Also a King scholar and disciple, Dyson writes that sexism prevented King from forging stronger connections with "radical black women who were his great ideological allies in the struggle against economic oppression."[12] Dyson makes the case for the deeply flawed and dynamically human Dr. King, lamenting the one-dimensionality of how we look at the man who has been frozen into an icon. Vincent Harding's book on Martin Luther King is far more gentle than the work of Dyson or Abernathy. Still, he wants to remind us that we cannot wrap the entire struggle for Black freedom around the person and persona of King: "The history of our struggle for the transformation of ourselves and this country, and the story of King's dream neither began nor ended in 1963. That seems simple, but it is not always easy to remember."[13] It has become even easier to remember in the twenty-first century, when we incessantly compare our contemporary freedom struggles to a lost past for which many are nostalgic. Rarely do we remember how unpopular King was at the time of his death. Seldom do we recall the breadth of his social justice vision. The chorus of "jobs, peace, and freedom" that was chanted during the 1963 March on Washington captures three of King's most pressing causes that he championed in the years before he died. By the time of his death, he understood the need for total transformation in the United States and the need for deep and lasting systemic change to purge the perpetuation of injustice.

Despite the public tendency to post or tweet famous quotations from King's works, it is important not to isolate his words from their original context. In the same speech in which we find *this*, we find *that*. For example: in the same essay in which he refers to

---

[11] Ralph David Abernathy, *And the Walls Came Tumbling Down: An Autobiography* (New York: HarperCollins, 1991).

[12] Dyson, *I May Not Get There with You*, 266.

[13] Harding, *Martin Luther King*, 48.

white brothers and sisters, he vociferously decries the sins of white supremacy. His is a both/and vision bursting with nuance. There are inherent contradictions to the cadence of his work. Others have already made the argument that we have reduced King to "a convenient icon shaped by our own distorted political images."[14] This reductive view extends to the works that we study in our limited King corpus.

There is no question that the sanitized, one-dimensional King does harm to how we are able to confront injustice. By looking closely at *The Trumpet of Conscience*, my goal is to offer an alternative that foregrounds the radical King and invites us not only to ruminate but to apply these parts of his vision to three contemporary social justice issues that have been shaping the twenty-first century. Even the ubiquitous "I Have a Dream" speech contains elements that are rarely reproduced and often overlooked in favor of the more sanitized version of King. Dyson encourages us to focus not only on the "dream" sentences but also the expressions of the pain and suffering of Black people that the speech conveys. For example, "There will be neither rest not tranquility in America until the Negro is granted his citizenship rights. The whirlwinds of revolt will continue to shake the foundations of our nation until the bright day of justice emerges." This remains true today. What if the people who critiqued today's Black Lives Matter protesters knew that King had made such a comment in his "I Have a Dream" speech?

Despite these shortcomings, there are things that I do admire about Rev. Dr. Martin Luther King. He was unquestionably a remarkable and prophetic visionary, a supremely gifted orator, a true social justice warrior, and a devoted lover of God. As a person of faith, I am unequivocally inspired by how his close walk with God led him to pursue justice. I am fascinated by what his prayer life reveals for the work of activism by people of faith and church communities. I am energized by his relentless focus on social justice that is the call of every follower of Jesus. But even while I respect and admire

---

[14]Dyson, *I May Not Get There with You*, 3.

the work that he did, I recognize that he is still flawed and fallible. Like Black feminist historian Barbara Ransby, I am aware that his infidelity asks that we take him down from the high pedestal, or at the very least be suspicious of his interactions with women.[15] To write about King is to write about how he has been remembered. But as noted earlier, I am less interested in writing about King as I am in writing about how his vision might inform and instruct us today. Like King, as a person of faith I struggle with the social and political dimensions of our world. Unlike King, as a Black feminist, I also invite women to the table as interlocutors and examples. The Black women I invoke in this book include King's better-known contemporaries like Fannie Lou Hamer and Ella Baker, and those who are lesser known like Prathia Hall, a young organizer and one of the first women to be ordained as a Baptist minister.

So where does this leave us? Dr. King was a flawed person and the way that we honor him is distorted. And these flaws are why annual celebrations of his life and legacy so often leave me feeling uncomfortable, largely because, for the most part, the man whom we celebrate today has been reduced to the author of a speech about dreams that children recite without reflection. He has been limited to snapshots of remembrance that do little to capture his complexity and gloss over the most radical parts of his vision. Too often, commemorating King means only remembering the parts of him that do not challenge us, the parts that make us comfortable, the parts that make us feel like we have achieved something because today little Black boys and little Black girls are able to join hands with little white boys and little white girls as sisters and brothers. Or that today, when I look at my own four children, I can name many of the times when they were seen by the content of their character rather than the color of their skin. We remember the parts that tell us we have made so much progress because not only is segregation (legally) over, but we have even had a Black president of the United States. These are the parts that comfort us as we enumerate how many monuments

---

[15]Barbara Ransby, "A Black Feminist's Response to Attacks on Martin Luther King Jr.'s Legacy," *New York Times*, June 3, 2019.

have been built in his name or how far we have come to dedicate a holiday to his life and legacy. But like the poem asserts, it is easier to build monuments than to build a better world, just as it is easier to reside in the comfort of "I Have a Dream" than to take King out of the box and wrestle with the more radical parts of his vision.

I am far from alone in my longing for appreciation of a more complex and radical Martin Luther King. Scholars—such as historian Vincent Harding, who was both King's friend and former speechwriter—have examined how MLK celebrations and commemorations suffer from what he calls historical amnesia. According to Harding, "Somehow it appeared as if we were determined to hold this hero captive to the powerful period of his life that culminated with the magnificent March on Washington of 1963, refusing to allow him to break beyond the stunning eloquence of 'I Have a Dream.'"[16] Disturbed by how King is "held captive," Harding, like Hines, probes the nuance—which is not to say that the stunning eloquence of "I Have a Dream" is not important. In fact, like many, I love King's "I Have a Dream" speech. It is a work of rhetorical perfection. I have fond memories of reciting it as a child and hearing clips of it over and over. It is truly a magnificent speech that showcases the talents of its orator. The idea of the dream is a profound leitmotif for any activist movement. I appreciate its symbolic resonance and its utility in framing visions of social justice. Dreams offer a different view in the world. Dreams are essential for what they impart about how we see the world beyond what is immediately apparent. Dreams reflect possibilities, alternative truths, preoccupations, and imaginations. The freedom to dream allows us to imagine freedom at its very core and essence. Dreams allow us to access something beyond language, the space where imagination and vision reign, and where anything becomes possible. Dreams, by their very definition, enable and activate our imaginations. Dreams are visions, goals, objectives, aims, hopes, intentions, desires, and yearnings, and we need these to build a better and different world. Notwithstanding my appreciation of the need to dream, now that I

---

[16]Harding, *Martin Luther King*, ix.

have my own school-age children, I have become that parent who wants them to know more about King than "I Have a Dream."

Vincent Harding explains that if we really want to recall King, we must recall him as he was. Like the Black Lives Matter founders and protesters, death loomed large in King's life. Death was ever-present. He "had to endure those deaths, more deaths, nightmare deaths," and he witnessed the deaths of people like John F. Kennedy, understanding what their implication meant in the fight against racial injustice.[17] Harding goes to great lengths to dispel the myths surrounding King, reminding the reader, for example, that "to re-call Martin is to re-call Malcolm. They were complementary and by the end of their lives, they knew it."[18] Harding's book is a moving meditation on King, written from the perspective of a friend who wonders if he ever knew the man whom he was so close to while they were alive. The book does not only critique the deification of King, it also serves as its own elegy and homage to a great man from his dear friend. Harding dwells on the prophetic nature of King's actions and vision. "Organizing, marching, singing the songs, standing unflinching before the blows, going to jail, challenging all the killers of dreams, he called us to sing, dream, and sign and build—and stand our ground, creating a new reality, a new nation, a new world, ready for the hero. He saw us dancing before we knew we could move. He recognized that we had not seen and was ready to live and die for it, for us."[19]

A RADICAL REVOLUTION OF VALUES

Dreaming encourages us to think and to imagine, in the words of the scholar Ashon Crawley, "otherwise." As he explains, "Otherwise possibility is the phrase I've been using to say that what we have is not all that is possible, that alternatives to the normative can exist,

---

[17]Harding, *Martin Luther King*, 7.
[18]Harding, *Martin Luther King*, 8.
[19]Harding, *Martin Luther King*, 35.

already exist in this world."[20] In other words, revolutionary dreams are a production of the "otherwise." Dreams offer an otherwise way to be in the world. Dreams are important for what they instruct about how we see the world beyond what is immediately in front of us. Dreams suggest myriad possibilities. The freedom to dream allows us to imagine what freedom might and can look like. Dreams allows us to access something beyond language: the space of imagination and vision, the ethereal where anything is possible. Dreams, by their very definition, enable our imaginations. When we yearn for social justice, something gets triggered that activates a desire to do and create. And as Toni Morrison reminds us, "The function of freedom is to free somebody else."[21] Our freedom should have a ripple effect. One of the effects of neoliberalism in the Black community, in particular, has been that we believe our freedom belongs to us and us alone. We are more concerned with personal freedoms than a collective, communal, and capacious vision. We have not used our freedom to set others free.

Compared to the speeches that King gave immediately before his death, the dreams that he outlines in his famous speech are far less radical. When he finally "broke his silence" on the war in Vietnam, or when he stood with the striking sanitation workers, or when he condemned the triple evils of "militarism, materialism, and white supremacy," the "I Have a Dream" speech looks benign in comparison. It is not a conspicuously radical text. It does not articulate some of the most controversial parts of his vision. They are not "revolutionary dreams." My use of the term "revolutionary dreams" comes first from Nikki Giovanni's poem of the same name.

> i used to dream militant
> dreams of taking
> over america to show

---

[20]Ashon T. Crawley, "It's Ok to Be Afraid," https://ashoncrawley.com [blog], March 16, 2020.

[21]Michael Andor Brodeur, "Toni Morrison in Her Own Words: 'The Function of Freedom Is to Free Someone Else,'" *Boston Globe*, August 6, 2019.

these white folks how it should be
done
i used to dream radical dreams
of blowing everyone away with my perceptive powers
of correct analysis
i even used to think i'd be the one
to stop the riot and negotiate the peace
then i awoke and dug
that if i dreamed natural
dreams of being a natural
woman doing what a woman
does when she's natural
i would have a revolution

In her poem, Nikki Giovanni takes the idea of the dream pro-
mulgated by King and turns it on its head. She outlines a liberatory
prise de conscience of a woman who begins with a narrow sense of
radicalism and grows to understand that simply being herself as a
woman, being who she is naturally, rather than adhering to typical
notions of what constitutes change, could further advance her desire
for revolution. By using the past tense, Giovanni implies two phases
of development—a past and a present, the latter ostensibly informed
by the former. Moving beyond where she was before, where she
"used to," allows the speaker to achieve a more complete, nuanced,
and balanced understanding of radical feminist politics. The promise
of revolution, Giovanni demonstrates, lies not only in the ability to
act but also in the ability and necessity to dream. The transformative power of dreaming teems with fundamental richness; the poem
encourages dreaming your own dreams. The incantation, "i used
to dream," followed by different iterations of political work that
prove to be intellectual, spiritual, activist, and racial, discloses just
how dreams, rather than deferred, can be short-circuited, hijacked,
or counterfeit unless they are our own. The poem's gorgeous conclusion suggests that maybe it is not the breadth of the dream that
matters, but rather the ability to dream in and of itself. Dreams are

important, Giovanni reminds us a few decades after Martin Luther King, but they are not the end of the story. What also matter are the quality and the texture of those dreams, and what we do with those dreams. Are they dreams that we work to transform into reality? Are they dreams that can build a better world? Or are they dreams that can quickly become nightmares?

What do we lose when we concentrate on the dream? And more practically, how do we move beyond the dream? Here we wrestle with those questions. King's later work, embodied by the collection *The Trumpet of Conscience*, provides a key to moving beyond the dream. In general, our sick society is far less comfortable with the more radical King. *The Trumpet of Conscience* also offers a revealing blueprint for what have become the defining social justice issues of our time. By taking the insights from those reflections as a point of departure for our dreams of freedom in the twenty-first century, we might discover how some of the most pressing social justice issues of our generation—racial justice, gender-based violence, and mass incarceration—might benefit from an analysis rooted in conscience.

The people who regularly cite the "I Have a Dream" speech probably do not know what King discloses in *The Trumpet of Conscience*—that "soon after speaking about the dream I saw it turn into a nightmare." When he makes this statement, he is referring to the conversations he has with poor Black people in the South as he realizes how attention to the dream is impossible without addressing the problem of class, and more specifically the elimination of poverty. But he could also be referring to how this speech has been co-opted today. In fact, as Dyson observes, "Out of sheer neglect, most of his other works have been cast aside as rhetorical stepchildren," perhaps because of the radical points contained therein.[22] Again, this is not to deny the significance of "I Have a Dream" as an oratorical masterpiece, as well as a singularly captivating moment in US history. Dreams, in and of themselves, are crucial entry points for the realization of justice.

---

[22]Dyson, *I May Not Get There with You*, 16.

As Nikki Giovanni explains in her poem, dreams are often where the work begins.

Some of the most telling examples of Dr. King as radical emerge at the end of his life. When in November and December 1967, the Canadian Broadcasting Corporation invited him to present a series of lectures, he took risks in the content that he had not previously embraced. King was told that he could speak on any topic that interested him and that was relevant to anyone in the world who might be listening. The series comprised five lectures and focused on topics that were close to his heart: nonviolent protest and civil disobedience, economic injustice, human rights for people of all races, and his opposition to the Vietnam War. Later on, it was published as *A Conscience for Change*, then *The Call to Conscience*, and it eventually reappeared as *The Trumpet of Conscience*. Each title is instructive. *A Conscience for Change* trains our eyes on the possibility of transformation. *The Call to Conscience* invokes a connection to a greater force and higher power beyond ourselves. *The Trumpet of Conscience* implores that we listen for and hear the spirit of our conscience. "The spirit is awake now; structures will follow, if we keep our ears open to the spirit."[23] In other words, as we look at issues of social justice, how can we better understand the imperative of conscience in making decisions about how to enact change? Alternatively described as "King's Call to Peace," these lectures are global in scope but gave focused attention to what he calls the triple American evils of racism, materialism, and militarism. *Racism* is a system or institution built on the perceived superiority of one group over another. *Militarism* refers to the United States' warmongering throughout the world. *Materialism* relates to the unfair production and distribution of resources in our society. Throughout these lectures, King laments the evils of racism, the scourge of poverty, and the horrors of war. He also extols the tireless work and creative contributions of youth organizers within the civil rights movement. Interestingly, King's profound understanding of

---

[23]King, *Trumpet of Conscience*, 51.

the global implications of the African American struggle made him one of the earliest US proponents of an international fight against anti-Blackness. King makes the point that movements for social change must internationalize to be effective. This global vision was vividly articulated long before his death in 1968. In fact, his trip to India as a pilgrim when he encountered the work of Mohandas Gandhi helped to determine his philosophy of nonviolence. King makes an explicit plea for Americans to sensitize themselves to the global march for justice. "I have said that the problem, the crisis that we face, is international in scope. In fact, it is inseparable from an international emergency which involves the poor, the dispossessed, and the exploited of the world."[24]

These were some of King's most controversial stances—his opposition to the war in Vietnam and his efforts to eradicate poverty in the United States. We can learn from his stance against the war: "I found myself obliged by conscience to end my silence and to take a public stance against my country's war in Vietnam."[25] The trumpet of conscience is one that breaks silence and decries every form of injustice. This is paramount because many people have forgotten King's attention to economic injustice and labor organizing. An appreciation of King that fails to acknowledge his stance on economic injustice is incomplete at best, and false at worst. Racial and economic justice are intertwined—one cannot function without the other. Taking King out of the box means asking how far we have come in addressing economic injustice. How is income inequality present in our lives today? Thinking about the rights of workers means caring about how a government shutdown affects people who are working without pay right now. It means taking on "the fight for fifteen" and advocating for doubling the minimum wage. It means caring about the essential workers who do not have the luxury of sheltering in place during a pandemic. Allowing the radical King to inspire our own justice work means adopting the view that "justice

---

[24]King, *Trumpet of Conscience*, 64.
[25]King, *Trumpet of Conscience*, 21.

is indivisible."[26] In other words, justice cannot be chopped into tiny slices with concerns about race here, concerns about justice there, and concerns about class somewhere else. As a Black feminist, my stance is that we cannot divide and parse out justice—all the different issues of social justice are intertwined. It means acknowledging that white supremacy is structural and institutional. It means believing in social change and having hope for the future. It means thinking globally and espousing a worldwide activism for peace. It means not remaining silent on pressing justice issues, no matter how controversial or inconvenient. *The Trumpet of Conscience* reveals King's commitment to a movement that went far beyond a single issue. Here we are reminded of Audre Lorde's wisdom: "We cannot build single-issue movements because we don't live single-issue lives." When Dr. King calls for a "radical revolution of values," it is "a true revolution of values [that looks] uneasily on the glaring contrast between poverty and wealth."[27] The radical King encourages innovation, urging his listeners to "find new ways to speak for peace."[28] The arguments made in the lectures are not easy to implement, nor do they lend themselves to catchy sound bites. They point to a more radical, unsettling vision that is rooted in conviction. Being unsettled is what the work of justice requires of us.

These speeches follow the same trajectory of speeches given later in King's life in which he asks important questions that can be instructive for our justice work today. For example, on the day before he died, his "I've Been to the Mountaintop" speech was given in support of striking sanitation workers in Tennessee, where he retells the story of the Good Samaritan and ends, as we noted in the introduction, by suggesting that whereas those who refused to stop along the way for the wounded man on the road ask, "If I stop to help this man, what will happen to me?" the Samaritan reverses this question: "If I do not stop to help this man, what will happen to him?" Rev. Dr. Martin Luther King queried in 1968, "If I do not

---

[26]King, *Trumpet of Conscience*, 24.
[27]King, *Trumpet of Conscience*, 32.
[28]King, *Trumpet of Conscience*, 33.

stop to help the sanitation workers, what will happen to them?" And today in 2020, we should also ask these kinds of questions: "If I do not stop to help families separated at the border, what will happen to them?"; "If I do not stop to help Syrian refugees, what will happen to them?"; "If I do not stop to help the housing insecure, what will happen to them?"; "If I do not stop to help the people on the migrant caravan, what will happen to them?"; "If I do not stop to help incarcerated people, what will happen to them?"; "If I do not stop to help survivors of rape and sexual assault, what will happen to them?"; and "If I do not stop to help #BlackLivesMatter activists, what will happen to them?" These were, effectively, King's last words. The speech he gave on the night before he died thus offers an important signpost pointing to where his vision would have gone had his life not ended abruptly at the age of thirty-nine. His messaging in that Christmas sermon was unequivocal:

> Our loyalties must transcend our race, our tribe, our class, and our nation; and this means we must develop a world perspective. . . . No individual can live alone; no nation can live alone, and as long as we try, the more we are going to have war in this world.[29]

In a speech condemning the Vietnam War, King declared:

> I speak for those whose land is being laid waste, whose homes are being destroyed, whose culture is being subverted. I speak for the poor of America who are paying the double price of smashed hopes at home and death and corruption in Vietnam. I speak as a citizen of the world, for the world as it stands aghast at the path we have taken. I speak as an American to the leaders of my own nation. The great initiative in this war is ours. The initiative to stop it must be ours.[30]

---

[29]Martin Luther King Jr., "Christmas Sermon," Ebenezer Baptist Church of Atlanta, Georgia, 1967.

[30]Martin Luther King Jr., "Conscience and the Vietnam War," in *The Lost Massey*

Whose land is being put to waste more today than the indigenous people of the United States? King never mentioned them in his speeches and essays; they were not the targets of his activism. He approached slavery as the original sin of the United States as opposed to the genocide of Native Americans, an oversight that today's social justice warriors know is inaccurate and incomplete.

MOVING BEYOND THE DREAM

Let us now move beyond the dream, or as I say, let's take King out of the box. To move beyond the dream, we must first learn about and celebrate those around Martin Luther King, especially women like Ella Baker and Fannie Lou Hamer. Describing King's acceptance speech for the Nobel Prize, Black feminist historian Barbara Ransby notes that he acknowledged that the prize was not only for him but for all who were actively engaging in the fight for civil rights. He referred to "the many people who make a successful journey possible, the known pilots and the unknown ground crew." These were people like Ella Baker, the organizer and activist who began as a field secretary for the National Association for the Advancement of Colored People (NAACP), then worked as an executive of the Southern Christian Leadership Conference (SCLC), and eventually influenced the founding of the Student Nonviolent Coordinating Committee (SNCC). A brilliant strategist committed to the process of change, Ella Baker espoused a theory of change with grassroots mass mobilization and action as its foundation. Explaining her role in the founding of SNCC, she once said, "You didn't see me on television, you didn't see news stories about me. The kind of role that I tried to play was to pick up pieces or put together pieces out of which I hoped organization might come. My theory is, strong people don't need strong leaders." This principle of organizing that privileges

---

Lectures: Recovered Classics from Five Great Thinkers (Toronto: House of Anansi, 2008), 185.

collectivity, community, and collaboration is also a Black feminist model. In fact, one of the ways that we trap King in a box is by disassociating him from "the vast numbers of women and men who constituted the very heart of the mid-twentieth-century US freedom movement."[31] Fond of charismatic male leaders, our society vaunts the individual over the collective. A look at Ella Baker's activism reveals that she was "deeply critical of a top-down, male-centered, charismatic model of leadership. It disempowered ordinary people, especially women and low-income and working-class people, and the power in collective organizing." She was a tireless organizer and strategist because she believed in freedom. Or, as she stated, "We who believe in freedom cannot rest." Scholar-activist and Baker biographer Barbara Ransby calls her "an insurgent intellectual with a passion for justice and democracy," explaining that "Ella Baker understood that laws, structures, and institutions had to change in order to correct injustice and oppression, but part of the process had to involve oppressed people, ordinary people, infusing new meanings into the concept of democracy and finding their own individual and collective power to determine their lives and shape the direction of history."[32] Baker's vision of democratic mass movement insisted on placing at the center those most affected by the struggle. Baker is also an example of the shortcomings of King's work and leadership practice as well as why we need to interrogate his legacy. She was uninhibitedly vocal about her exclusion from the SCLC, as were many Black women during the civil rights movement. Too often, the role of women in the movement was prescriptive and reductive; as Ransby notes, in many political organizations, "women were indispensable but underappreciated."[33] The way we remember the movement often overlooks the contributions of many Black women who should be recognized for their activism, organizing, and leadership.

When we examine other, relatively marginal figures of the civil

---

[31] Angela Y. Davis, *Freedom Is a Constant Struggle* (Chicago: Haymarket, 2016), 2.

[32] Ransby, *Ella Baker*, 1.

[33] Ransby, *Ella Baker*, 106.

rights movement, a different model of activism and social justice emerges. This version is collective and communal rather than narrowly focused on one person. For example, when we acknowledge the Black women and girls involved in the bus boycotts before Rosa Parks—or we choose to move beyond the distorted and narrow view regarding Parks herself—we clear space for appreciating the groundbreaking interventions of others. Fifteen-year-old Claudette Colvin is an important example who is often left out of official histories on how the Montgomery bus boycotts unfolded. Colvin quietly refused to give up her seat while riding the bus one day and was jailed for doing so. In the book *Claudette Colvin: Twice toward Justice*, Colvin explains the history of her involvement in civil rights in general and the Montgomery bus boycotts specifically. In 1955, at the age of fifteen, she refused to give up her seat on the bus but the historical record has not remembered her. The story of Claudette Colvin also affirms the overarching desire for sanitized heroes with which I have been wrestling.

To move beyond the dream, we must also anchor our fight for justice in something greater than ourselves. The cause of freedom for all is not enough in and of itself to inspire, motivate, and sustain. One of the questions that my students most frequently ask is how to maintain hope and still have joy in the face of injustice. Bryan Stevenson, the founder and executive director of the Equal Justice Initiative, a human rights organization in Montgomery, Alabama, and a trailblazing civil rights lawyer, says that "hopelessness is the enemy of justice."[34] If indeed hopelessness is the enemy of justice, how do we remain hopeful in the face of widespread injustice? Where can we look for hope? Faith, collectivity, and joy are the sources of hope that I encourage my students to pursue as they endeavor to remain anchored and encouraged in their justice work. We can activate joy as a form of resistance. To be clear, when I refer to *joy*, I am not talking about happiness. I am talking about a

---

[34]Bryan Stevenson, *Just Mercy: A Story of Justice and Redemption* (New York: Spiegel & Grau, 2014), 160.

deep well that extends beyond positive emotions and allows us to commune with a power far greater than ourselves. I also understand joy as a fruit of the spirit, which means that being close to God and the divine brings joy. At the end of her novel *Possessing the Secret of Joy*, Alice Walker writes, "Resistance is the secret of joy."[35] It is also true that "joy is the secret of resistance." In other words, joy can (and should) fuel and inspire our activism. This is why justice warriors like the antirape activist and founder of the Me Too movement Tarana Burke describes the need to curate joy and anchor the fight against sexual violence in her hope for the future.

Social justice movements that move beyond individual needs and imagine the importance of systemic change broaden their reach. The collective can also be a source of hope. As Angela Davis explains, "It is in collectivities that we find reservoirs of hope and optimism."[36] Along with the hope that comes from working in a collective manner and curating joy, faith is a deep well from which we can draw to gird us in the struggle for justice and freedom. Dr. Martin Luther King gave us a powerful model of a faith that does justice. For him, social justice was a moral imperative that was rooted in his dynamic faith in God, an example of how *conviction* and *calling* go hand in hand. He was able to do this work as he did because of his faith.

For me, the best definition of faith can be found in the Letter to the Hebrews: "Faith is the assurance of things hoped for, the conviction of things not seen" (11:1). Faith is what we see at work in King's final speech, "I've Been to the Mountaintop," in which he demonstrates his belief in the unseen and declares: "I've seen the promised land. I may not get there with you. But I want you to know . . . that we, as a people, will get to the promised land." The idea that justice would eventually come regardless of whether he was there to witness it is born from faith. To move beyond the dream, we must ask ourselves how to build a society in which racial justice is at the center, not merely an ornament or a yearly event.

---

[35] Alice Walker, *Possessing the Secret of Joy* (New York: Washington Square Press, 1992).
[36] Davis, *Freedom Is a Constant Struggle*, 49.

Furthermore, King's prayers reveal how earnestly he prayed for strength to lead the movement and for God's justice to prevail. They also show the extent to which prayer was a lifeline that kept him tethered to God. He prayed for endurance, protection, greater vision, mercy, and humility. One prayer in particular that is striking is, "O God, help me to see myself in my true perspective. Help me, O God, to see that I'm just a symbol of a movement . . . and that a boycott would have taken place in Montgomery, Alabama, if I had never come to Alabama. Help me to realize that I am because of the forces of history and because of the fifty thousand Negroes of Alabama who will never get their names in the papers and in the headlines. O God, help me to see that where I stand today, I stand because others helped me to stand there and because the forces of history projected me there. And this moment would have come in history even if M. L. King had never been born."[37] King's expansive view of the world, combined with his belief in a God of justice, enabled him to appreciate his place in the movement even when others did not and still do not. What if we were to approach his legacy with the same kind of informed humility?

These prayers are especially moving because they reveal the importance of empathy in advancing the work of social justice. As I write this in 2020—as the pandemic upends and ravages people's lives, locking their lungs and preventing them from breathing—I sit comfortably in my home with my four children who are playing or doing schoolwork. Our days are long, but our circumstances are far from dire. I cry every day because I keep thinking about people who are without health insurance and the homeless people who cannot shelter in place because they have no shelter. My heart is broken for people who live in violent homes with their perpetrators for whom home is neither a shelter nor a refuge. I am concerned for people who have lost their jobs as a result of this crisis and must wonder if they will ever work again, and if so when. My heart is broken

---

[37]Martin Luther King Jr., "Conquering Self-Centeredness," sermon delivered at Dexter Avenue Baptist Church, Montgomery, Alabama, August 11, 1957, http://okra.stanford.edu.

for the hundreds of thousands of people who have died in the pandemic and their loved ones who continue to mourn their loss. I am enraged that even while the entire country seems to have come to a standstill, there are still people dying violent deaths as a result of anti-Blackness. I am encouraged by King's prayers, because he also knew exactly where to place prayer in relation to action, something that the church does not do as well today. King's understanding that faith without works is dead informed how he participated in the freedom movement. "As a minister I take prayer too seriously to use it as an excuse for avoiding work and responsibility. When a government commands more wealth and power than has even been known in the history of the world, and offers no more than this, it is worse than blind, it is provocative."[38]

As a college professor at a Jesuit university for more than a decade, I have had many moving, difficult, and meaningful conversations with students on the topic of justice and their role as young people. Many of these conversations are about the challenge of still having to fight racism on campus. Their despair and fatigue are real—and they worry that they may not get to see the fruits of their labor. I encourage my students to draw strength from the models of those who came before them and who were faced with more dire circumstances, like King and many others—like the enslaved Africans of colonial Saint-Domingue who fought against the French during the Haitian Revolution, a thirteen-year battle for independence. Even one of the most renowned Haitian revolutionaries, Toussaint Louverture, died before the dream of independence was realized. In the famous, apocryphal phrase that Louverture is said to have uttered while boarding the ship to his captivity before his death, he spoke prophetically about the successful end of the revolution. Referring to himself as the "Tree of Liberty," he claimed that "in capturing me you have cut down the tree of liberty, but its roots are deep."[39]

Like Ella Baker, I am inspired and energized by college students

---

[38]King, *Trumpet of Conscience*, 61.
[39]Toussaint Louverture, Toussaint Louverture Historical Society, http://toussaintlouverturehs.org.

and other young people committed to working for justice. This work cannot be done without them. They must lead, and we must listen to their voices. For the generation of students with whom we are privileged to work, the despair can be real, but should not be an end point. As my colleague and sociologist Shawn McGuffey and I remind our students, to nurture your activism, you have to make space for and seek out joy.

In his study of King, Vincent Harding ultimately concludes that "perhaps each generation must forge its own understanding of King's meaning, must determine and demonstrate the power of his impact and influence for our lives." It is incumbent upon us to ask, What is ours? Is it to keep King in a box? Is it to limit ourselves to the "I Have a Dream" speech? Is it to embrace the radical King? Is it to ponder seriously, only once a year in January, the questions he posed? Is it to heed the blowing horn of the trumpet? Is it to sing hosannas to his name? Or is it to build a better world?

2

Ending Racism

If we do not stop to help the #BlackLivesMatter activists, what will become of them?

BLACK LIVES MATTER

Black lives matter.
Black lives matter.
All Black lives matter.
Black women's lives matter.
 Black nonbinary lives matter.
Black men's lives.
Black trans' lives matter.
Black girls' lives matter.
Black boys' lives matter.
Black children's lives matter.
Our lives matter.
All Black lives matter.
Black lives matter.

This refrain should never be taken lightly. It is a sacred refrain. It is a statement that is also a rallying cry. It is an affirmation of life and a declaration that, even though racism is the air that we breathe, our breath is sacred. This refrain is a call, a cry, a communal response, a reflection, and an invitation. The statement "Black Lives Matter" represents one of the most important utterances about the proliferation of racial injustice in the twenty-first century. It is a simple affirmation whose necessity reveals the kind of world in which we live. To understand and embrace that *all Black lives do matter* is to appreciate intersectionality—the idea that oppressions overlap and exacerbate one another—and to comprehend the depths of the struggle against anti-Black racism in the United States and abroad. When we say that Black lives matter, we affirm Black life and recognize a humanity that has too often been denied throughout history to the present day. Radical dignity and common humanity sit at the foundation of the Black Lives Matter movement. It should not be necessary to note, but given the continuous cycle of anti-Black violence, racist abuse, and the stronghold of white supremacy in this country, "Black lives matter" needs to be explicitly articulated. At the most basic level, the Black Lives Matter movement has emerged as a response to the dehumanization of Black people. The fact that too often, Black humanity and dignity do not seem to matter in the face of state-sanctioned violence makes it necessary for us to say, "Black lives matter"; to scream, "Black lives matter'"; to teach, "Black lives matter"; and to cry, "Black lives matter" again and again.

AN ETHIC OF LOVE

Alicia Garza first used the phrase "Black Lives Matter" on July 13, 2013, after the acquittal of George Zimmerman. In a love letter to Black people, she wrote, "We don't deserve to be killed with impunity. . . . Black people, I love you. I love us. We matter. Our lives matter."[1] Black Lives Matter. It was a love letter that launched a movement. What does it mean to say that love was the genesis

---

[1] Alicia Garza, *The Purpose of Power: How We Come Together When We Fall Apart* (New York: One World, 2020), 125.

of Black Lives Matter? In other words, how does our view of the movement shift when we recognize that love is its foundation? It is actually not a far leap. According to theologian and public intellectual Cornel West, we must "never forget that justice is what love looks like in public."[2] Led by an abiding love for all of humanity, the founders of the Black Lives Matter movement have worked hard to make sure that the "lives of Black people are just as valuable as the lives of others."[3]

In 2020, after the murder of George Floyd, protests occurred in all fifty states as well as in many countries around the world. The Black Lives Matter movement reached a fever pitch of recognition. According to the *New York Times*, Black Lives Matter was the largest movement in US history, with nearly twenty-six million people having participated in protests in 2020.[4] While Black Lives Matter protests are now known to many, it is more than a phrase to chant or a sign to place on your lawn. What began as simply a hashtag evolved into a movement and has now expanded into an international organization with chapters around the world campaigning and leading the charge to decry and eliminate anti-Black racism. But "Black Lives Matter" is also an ethic and a call to action. Black Lives Matter advances a policy platform that includes concrete actions and suggestions for defunding the police and prison abolition. As described by the creators of the movement, Black Lives Matter is an *ideology* and an *intervention*: "an ideological and political intervention in a world where Black lives are systemically and intentionally targeted for demise. It is an affirmation of Black folks' humanity, our contributions to this society, and our resilience in the

---

[2] Cornel West, "The caravan of love is flowing, and never forget that love is what justice looks like in public, just like tenderness is what love feels like in private," October 22, 2020, https://www.facebook.com/drcornelwest/posts/in-this-unprecedented-election-build-on-the-best-of-those-who-came-before-you-li/10164237879340111/.

[3] Alicia Garza, "Dear Mama Harriet," in *Radical Hope: Letters of Love and Dissent in Dangerous Times*, ed. Carolina de Robertis (New York: Vintage, 2017), 20.

[4] Larry Buchanan, "Black Lives Matter May Be the Largest Movement in U.S. History," *New York Times*, June 6, 2020.

face of deadly oppression."[5] Black Lives Matter is thus, a network, a movement, an ideology, and an intervention intended to transform minds, systems, and societies.

A few days after publishing her love letter to Black people on social media, Alicia Garza reflected further on what it means to say, "Black lives matter." She wrote,

> #BlackLivesMatter is a collective affirmation and embracing of the resistance and resilience of Black people. It is a reminder and a demand that our lives be cherished, respected, and able to access our full dignity and determination. It is a truth that we are called to embrace if our society is to become human again. It is a rallying cry. It is a prayer. The impact of embracing and defending the value of Black life has the potential to lift us all. #Blacklivesmatter asserts the truth of Black life that collective action builds collective power for collective transformation.[6]

What we know today is that the Black Lives Matter (BLM) movement began in 2013 with the combined efforts of three Black women activists from different backgrounds. Patrisse Cullors, Opal Tometi, and Alicia Garza were living in California and working together to create the movement and to secure the future of Black people in an antiracist world. Two of the women are queer, one is of Nigerian descent. I mention their backgrounds because it is relevant that, although Black Lives Matter became known mostly through the symbolic importance of Black men who were killed by police, the women who began the movement did not intend for that to be its main objective. They always understood the movement to represent all Black lives globally, whether those people are women, nonbinary, men, transgender, or children. The history of BLM makes clear that, if we are to understand the movement properly, we must see it as an intervention as well as an ideology that is robustly intersectional.

---

[5] See https://blacklivesmatter.com/herstory.
[6] Garza, *Purpose of Power,* 120.

As historian Jelani Cobb explains regarding Garza's initial Facebook post, "The post was intended as an affirmation for a community distraught over George Zimmerman's acquittal in the shooting death of seventeen-year-old Trayvon Martin, in Sanford, Florida. A seasoned activist, Garza has worked for organizations such as the National Domestic Workers Alliance, which represents twenty thousand caregivers and housekeepers, and lobbies for labor legislation on their behalf. She is also an advocate for queer and transgender rights and for anti-police-brutality campaign."[7] In that love letter, Garza writes from the heart: "I continue to be surprised at how little Black lives matter. And I will continue that. Stop giving up on Black life. . . . Black people, I will never give up on us. I love you. I love us. Our lives matter."[8]

Openly registering her own surprise that Zimmerman would not be held accountable for the murder of Trayvon Martin, Garza refused to capitulate to the notion that the outcome was to be expected because Black people's lives do not matter. She urged others to refuse to be indifferent to the loss of Black life and resolved to be surprised every time someone was found not guilty of killing a Black person. Garza's gesture acknowledges the weariness that racism foists onto Black and Brown people, causing us to respond to police brutality with comments like "I am not surprised," or "What did you expect?"

Our experience of anti-Black racism in the United States has resulted in chronic fatigue and the expectation that Black lives will never be valued. When yet another police officer is acquitted—or not even charged, as was the case for Breonna Taylor—for killing one of us, we say that we are not surprised because we do not expect justice to be realized for Black people. We do not expect for anyone beyond ourselves to value Black life. We expect the majority to see our lives as disposable. Alicia Garza cautions that this kind of response is dangerous and can be tantamount to giving up on Black lives. In response to rampant and unchecked police,

[7]Jelani Cobb, "The Matter of Black Lives," *New Yorker*, March 7, 2016.
[8]Garza, *Purpose of Power,* 111.

state, and vigilante killings of unarmed Black people, BLM holds and upholds Black life.

Responding to Garza's post, her friend and fellow activist Patrisse Cullors then turned the three words—Black Lives Matter—into a hashtag and circulated it on social media. The use of the hashtag exploded within a few hours of its original posting. Over the next few days, Garza and Cullors added Opal Tometi to their initial organizing to create a website and social media accounts for Black Lives Matter. Describing these humble beginnings Cullors writes, "I hope it impacts more than we can ever imagine."[9] In the book *Making All Black Lives Matter,* Black feminist historian Barbara Ransby charts the history of the movement, focusing on "the set of conditions and circumstances that set the stage for the movement to emerge."[10] As Ransby explains, while Black Lives Matter began with Garza's letter, it was followed by Cullors's response on social media, and then forever transformed in 2014 by the Ferguson uprising in response to the killing of Michael Brown. The movement is rooted in a tradition of Black feminist organizing that takes seriously the need for collaboration and privileges and an intersectional view of social justice.

This history indicates that although it is not often mentioned in the public discourse, *love* was the origin of Black Lives Matter. The movement was born of love, advances love, and issues a call for love that can also remind us of Martin Luther King. Garza's grief for her beloved Black community inspired her to write that love letter. As an activist, Garza's uncomplicated affirmation of Black life was intended to encourage, inspire, heal, and repair. It was an affirmation of Blackness and Black life imbued with a healing and sacred power. It evolved from a mere slogan to become what has been called "a battle cry of this generation of Black youth activists."[11]

---

[9]Patrisse Khan-Cullors and asha bandele, *When They Call You a Terrorist: A Black Lives Matter Memoir* (New York: St. Martin's Griffin, 2017), 181.

[10]Barbara Ransby, *Making All Black Lives Matter: Reimagining Freedom in the 21st Century* (Oakland: University of California Press, 2008), 11.

[11]Ransby, *Making All Black Lives Matter*, 1.

The fact that this movement was founded as an act of love suggests that it fits into a long trajectory of justice motivated by love that also animated Dr. King's activism. Love was at the center of King's philosophy and undergirded his practice of nonviolence. As he stated, "It's so basic to me because it is a part of my basic philosophical and theological orientation: the whole idea of love, the whole philosophy of love."[12] For King, love is essential and fundamental because "only love will save our civilization."[13] Love is the only way. It is impossible to overstate the centrality of love in the writings and work of Martin Luther King. Love was central to his theology, philosophy, vision, teachings, and activism. For King, as for Alicia Garza and her fellow founders of Black Lives Matter, justice begins with love. Yet somehow, the public conversation around Black Lives Matter has repeatedly failed to connect it to love. In fact, efforts to distance the work of the BLM movement from King's legacy identify the latter's call to love as the most glaring distinction between them.

In addition to being a movement birthed in love, BLM stands as a twenty-first-century example of where youth and social action combine in the fight for racial justice. Black Lives Matter is an intervention with explicit policy demands. There is no question that Black Lives Matter has transformed and informed the lives of an entire generation. The average young person of high school and college age today has not only heard of the movement but has also attended a Black Lives Matter protest. These young people came of age just as the movement was beginning. Rarely has a year passed in their lives when Black Lives Matter protests did not erupt. In other words, rarely did a year go past that a Black person was not killed by police or vigilantes. Sadly, the daily police killings of people in the United States continue unchecked. Black Lives Matter progressed from being a local movement against racist policing to

---

[12]Martin Luther King Jr., "Loving Your Enemies," sermon delivered at Dexter Avenue Baptist Church, Montgomery, Alabama, November 17, 1957, http://okra. stanford.edu.

[13]King, "Loving Your Enemies."

a global movement with the dignity and humanity of Black people at its center. The larger Movement for Black Lives (M4BL) pursues policy changes in order to hold police accountable and to defund the police. When the founders of #BLM announced their platform in 2016, "A Vision for Black Lives: Policy Demands for Power, Freedom, and Justice," they explained that the movement was about both grassroots action and systemic change. The international eruption of Black Lives Matter protests in 2020 further confirms that the movement is global. When we say all Black lives matter, we mean Black lives all over the world, because anti-Blackness is an international phenomenon.

While the Black Lives Matter movement does have specific policy-related recommendations, their vision not only focuses on changing the law but also advances a view toward a more just society in which systems and structures of power can be overturned. The vision is thus both practical and theoretical. The idea that Black dignity can be reclaimed for all signals a change that must take place in the culture, not only in laws and policies. Martin Luther King had a similar perspective. As much as he fought for desegregation and was a proponent of laws like the Civil Rights Act and the Voting Rights Act, he understood that laws alone could not transition us into a world where Black life actually matters: "By now it is obvious that new laws are not enough," he writes in the chapter, "Non-Violence as a National Strategy."[14] In his call for more than new laws, King encourages a Black freedom movement that is both ideology and intervention—along the lines of the Black Lives Matter movement.

Youth and Social Action

As a window into seeing how a new generation is organizing against racial injustice in the twenty-first century, the Black Lives Matter movement connects well to *The Trumpet of Conscience.* The importance of youth in movements against injustice cannot be

---

[14]King, *Trumpet of Conscience*, 56.

contested, especially when we consider the necessity of creating legacies that can be institutionalized and sustained over generations. Martin Luther King devotes an entire chapter to the topic of youth and social action, in which he decries "the alienation of young people from society" and argues that the "unprecedented attitudes" of that generation exist because "this generation was born and matured in unprecedented conditions."[15] The same can be said of this generation of young people today, many of whom I have the pleasure of interacting with regularly in my profession and my work as an activist. This generation—whom the poet Elizabeth Alexander has dubbed "The Trayvon Generation"—are young people who have come of age with moving images of Black deaths as a constant backdrop. Barely teenagers when Trayvon Martin was killed by George Zimmermann in 2012, those who entered college in 2014 would have been classmates of Michael Brown had he not been killed by police in Ferguson at the age of eighteen. Those who entered college in fall 2020 were the same age as Tamir Rice, who was only twelve years old when a police officer killed him, and might have been his college classmates had he lived. They are young people like the youth leaders of A Long Walk Home in Chicago, who have been upholding and organizing around the memory of Rekia Boyd since her death in 2012. They are the ones to whom Alicia Garza wrote her love letter, encouraging them not to lose hope or succumb to indifference. Many of them were able to vote for the first time in 2016, when they witnessed the ascent of a racist, misogynistic, xenophobic, and homophobic man to the highest office of the most powerful country in the world.

As these young people are often fond of proclaiming, this is not the movement of their grandparents. They are different from their ancestors who participated in the civil rights movement. For the young people of today, freedom begins with the imagination. They distinguish themselves from previous generations because, in their minds, the elders were not radical enough. Radical imaginations

---

[15]King, *Trumpet of Conscience*, 37–38.

demand the impossible, the kind of impossible that James Baldwin describes in *The Fire Next Time*: "I know what I'm asking is impossible. But in our time, as in every time, the impossible is the least that one can demand—and one is, after all, emboldened by the spectacle of human history in general, and the American Negro history in particular, for it testifies to nothing less than the perpetual achievement of the impossible."[16]

Clearly, there are significant differences between this generation of young people and the young people whom King referred to in the 1960s when he wrote "Youth and Social Action." But despite some of the marked, often stark differences, some similarities are also worth noting that are rarely explored. For example, many of today's young people indeed belong to "a new breed of radicals," similar to those whom King described over fifty years ago. "All of them agree that only by structural change can current evils be eliminated, because the roots are in the system rather than in [people] or in faulty operation. They are a new breed of radicals."[17] This generation espouses "cancel culture," which many people of the previous generations disdained and openly critiqued. Still, my concern is that the call to cancel "cancel culture" takes on the same tactics that those who critique it are hoping to dismiss. We have to take young people seriously and engage them where they are in the work because they are the future. We must take the Ella Baker approach to organizing that trusts them to find the way. They are also impatient as they wait for change. And rightfully so.

During the 1960s King witnessed "heightened black impatience and stiffened white resistance" as two sides of a coin adding another layer of difficulty to the struggle against racial injustice.[18] In the twenty-first century that impatience is even more profound as we witness a generation that cannot and should not have to wait.

Martin Luther King was often critical, but never dismissive, of young people during his movement leadership. His relationship to

---

[16]James Baldwin, *The Fire Next Time* (New York: Vintage, 1994), 104.

[17]King, *Trumpet of Conscience*, 40.

[18]King, *Trumpet of Conscience*, 15.

the Student Nonviolent Coordinating Committee illustrates this dynamic. According to Stokely Carmichael, "Of all the adult leaders, Dr. King had always best understood and supported SNCC's work."[19] Nevertheless, despite the fact that he supported the SNCC's work from the beginning and was excited that it began as a student-led initiative, King's relationship to this group was often contentious. There were nonetheless those like John Lewis and other SNCC members who surrounded him in the fight against racial injustice. His relationship with Lewis is a beautiful example of an intergenerational partnership that is essential for social movements to flourish. While their relationship has been lauded as a model for intergenerational collaboration—especially in the wake of John Lewis's recent death—people are less familiar with some of their tensions. Those tensions are important because they help to highlight that the youth during the civil rights movement did not always agree with King's leadership.

"A New Breed of Radicals"

King's reference to the youth as "a new breed of radicals," whose interests were not always cohesive or united, was intended to be a critique, but in 2020 we can reclaim this language and apply it to the Black Lives Matter movement. In this century, our own "new breed of radicals" deploys the language and the insights of intersectionality to demand the impossible. They activate their radical imaginations to generate a vision of change. They are well represented by progressives like Alexandria Ocasio-Cortez, who amplifies how race, gender, and class intersect in her experience as a member of Congress. While their belief in the impossible is not new, the means they use to realize it are. In over a decade of teaching a class on Black feminism to college students at a Jesuit institution, I have noticed each year the growth of my students in knowledge and wisdom. Whereas years ago, reading Kimberlé Crenshaw's

---

[19]See https://snccdigital.org/people/martin-luther-king-jr/.

1989 article in which she first uses the term *intersectionality* was a major feat for my students, today many of them know the term before coming to my class and are familiar with its intricate theory.[20] They are imagining and attempting to create a world that is free for all people, regardless of their race, class, sexuality, gender, or ability. They realize that "injustice anywhere is a threat to justice everywhere."[21] But unlike the young people whom King said "are in serious revolt against old values and have not yet concretely formulated the new ones," today's student activists and organizers have concrete plans. Many of them espouse the policy suggestions put forth in the Black Lives Matter platform: they want to defund the police, they want prison abolition, and they want an entirely new system of government for the United States. They are like the students I taught in the spring of 2020 who were set apart, bound to be special as a result of the pandemic.

Those students began college in 2016, when many of them voted for the first time in what was one of the most contentious elections of a generation. Only a few months after arriving on campus, they had to face the fact that this country elected someone who is perhaps the antithesis of the values that a liberal arts education espouses. Most of their college career was under the leadership of a president who has done more to fan into flame than discourage various forms of hatred—misogyny, racism, sexism, ableism, homophobia, transphobia, xenophobia, Islamophobia, and anti-Semitism—and the normalizing of all of this exposed the depth and the contours of the sickness ailing American society. The stratifications of race, class, gender, ability, and sexual orientation that regulate our society have blinded us to the way of love and deepened those divisions.

As a person of faith, a Black woman, a feminist, a mother, and a

---

[20]Kimberlé Crenshaw, "Demarginalizing the Intersection of Race and Sex: A Black Feminist Critique of Antidiscrimination Doctrine, Feminist Theory and Antiracist Politics," *University of Chicago Legal Forum* 140 (1989): 139–67.

[21]Martin Luther King Jr., April 16, 1963, "Letter from a Birmingham Jail," www.stanford.edu/group/King/popular_requests/frequentdocs/birmingham.pdf.

professor, I remember that day in November quite vividly and the sense that something had shifted on college campuses. I recall the Black Muslim student who came into my office and wept as she shared her fear that she would be attacked because of her religion. I remember abandoning my teaching plan for the day to offer time and space for my students to share their thoughts about the election. Most of the students in my class—twenty women and one man—were dumbfounded. After class was dismissed, a few stayed behind and wept. One shared with me, "I took my friend to the ER last week because she was raped, and now. . . ." She didn't complete her sentence, but I already understood. As someone who has spent so much of my life working with and advocating for rape survivors, it pained me to think that someone who so publicly embodied, endorsed, and perpetuated rape culture would now hold the highest office in the land. But what I saw in the young people I work with during the months and years following the election inspired me. Students were more committed than ever to making their voices heard, becoming civically engaged, and advancing social justice causes. They were organized and strategic in their efforts, consistently backing up their vision of a more just world with policies to implement it.

One of the recurring problems that critics of Black Lives Matter have with the movement is an inability to identify a single (and usually male) leader or figurehead at the helm. As Alicia Garza makes clear, that is precisely the point. This choice is an intentional outgrowth of the Black feminism that the BLM founders espouse. Today's young activists operate from a model of shared, collective, and collaborative power that is purposefully nonhierarchical. In *Making All Black Lives Matter*, Barbara Ransby comments on this generation's explicit and deliberate departure from a singular model of leadership, explaining that this movement "has patently rejected the hierarchical hetero-patriarchal politics of respectability. Organizers have eschewed values that privilege the so-called best and brightest, emphasizing the needs of the most marginal and often-maligned sectors of the Black community. . . . This is the first time in the history of social movements that Black feminist politics have defined the frame for a multi-issue, Black-led mass struggle that did not primarily or exclusively focus on women."[22] Although we live in a culture that privileges the model of a single, usually male, leader to be seen as the face and voice of our freedom movements—and it is very much into this tradition that our memorialization of King is inscribed—shared and collaborative leadership is a much more common and often effective organizing model. Ransby notes that King tried to acknowledge as much when he accepted the Nobel Peace Prize in 1964: "When the Rev. Dr. Martin Luther King Jr. accepted the Nobel Peace Prize in Oslo in 1964, he observed that anytime an award is given to 'the dedicated pilots of our struggle who have sat at the controls as the freedom movement soared into orbit,' the prize is also bestowed on 'the ground crew without whose labor and sacrifices the jet flights to freedom could never have left the earth.'"[23] Speaking prophetically once again, it was as though King knew that history would remember him and elevate his name over the hundreds of other everyday people in the struggle for Black freedom.

In their effort to advance a Black-led mass freedom movement, BLM activists supplant and transform the power structures of King's generation. To reimagine how power functions in our society, we have to be willing to shift the centers of power. The Black Lives Matter movement's use of mass protest has, in fact, become what King called "a new stage of struggle [that] can transmute the deep rage of the ghetto into a constructive and creative force."[24] This is rage channeled into productive action. The power of this constructive and creative force is clear when we consider how many people have participated in these protests. This century is also proving that Black Lives Matter can have a reach into government as well, as the election of Cori Bush in 2020 demonstrates. Like Jesus Christ

[22]Ransby, *Making All Black Lives Matter*, 3.
[23]Barbara Ransby, "Ella Baker's Legacy Runs Deep, Know Her Name," *New York Times*, January 20, 2020.
[24]King, *Trumpet of Conscience*, 16.

himself, King was not against anger and rage. He understood that what John Lewis called "good trouble" often stemmed from feelings like anger and rage against injustice.

Despite the derision directed toward the Black Lives Matter movement and the negative comparisons between BLM and the civil rights movement, these movements *for Black freedom* have more in common than is widely known in the popular imagination. Even as it attempts to improve upon some of the work done in the 1950s and 1960s, the Black Lives Matter movement also draws inspiration from the 1960s actions, demonstrated by the Freedom Rides in support of the Ferguson uprising in 2014: "The Black Lives Matter Freedom Ride was designed to gather Black people from other parts of the country to go to St. Louis and support the Black people who were being attacked and maligned by the state for standing up for their right to live with dignity."[25] As one of the first national initiatives of the Black Lives Matter movement, the Freedom Rides exemplified that this new generation was aware of the history of resistance to anti-Black racism in the United States and committed to building on those practices as they continued the struggle.

Notwithstanding my view that King would support the Black Lives Matter movement, just as his mentee John Lewis often did, it is worth noting some of the distinctions between this movement in the twenty-first century and the Black freedom movement of the 1960s. Along with their rejection of a model of masculine leadership and monolithic hierarchy, a clear area of difference is that King was adamant about the need for negotiation, whereas the current platform for Black Lives Matter does not make room for anything less than meeting demands to uphold Black dignity and humanity. King expressed that need for negotiation: "Life and history give eloquent testimony to the fact that conflicts are never resolved without useful give-and-take on both sides."[26] Certainly, Martin Luther King was never against protest. He encouraged it and urged every citizen to

---

[25]Garza, *Purpose of Power*, 125.
[26]King, *Trumpet of Conscience*, 22.

know how to participate. "Every [person] of humane convictions must decide on the protest that best suits his [or her] convictions, but we must all protest."[27] By telling people to find the form of protest that suits them, King established his support of a long-standing tradition in the Black freedom struggle.

Black Lives Matter began as a love letter shared on social media, circulated as a popular hashtag, and ignited a fully fledged global movement with a plan of action and a strategic platform. Much of this action was inspired by the death of Black men and boys and the subsequent nonindictment of their killers. When Michael Brown was killed by police and left to die in the middle of the street in Ferguson, local organizers immediately began to mobilize in protest of his death. In other words, as Ransby notes, "If the police murder of Michael Brown in Ferguson in summer of 2014 was the fire that signaled the full-blown emergence of the Black Lives Matter Movement and the Movement for Black Lives, then the vigilante murder with impunity of Trayvon Martin in Sanford, Florida, in February 2012 was the spark."[28] That spark has transformed an entire generation, forcing them to bear witness to the death of so many unarmed Black people at the hands of vigilantes and police.

A Local and Global Movement

While the greater Movement for Black Lives began in response to the police, state, and vigilante violence against Black people in the United States, it is also a global movement. Although in the United States it has been mostly seen as local and domestic, the founders of the Black Lives Matter movement have always espoused a global vision. This is why an essential part of the BLM strategy is the structure of local chapters, each with its own autonomy to act locally and determine what is best for the communities in which they live. These Black visionary activists understand and exemplify

---

[27]King, *Trumpet of Conscience*, 32.
[28]Ransby, *Making All Black Lives Matter,* 29.

King's point that "the conscience of an awakened activist cannot be satisfied with a focus on local problems, if only because he sees that local problems are all interconnected with world problems."[29] The movement has taken root in Latin America and on the African continent as well as in Europe. In Nigeria the #EndSARS movement against police brutality champions the vision of Black Lives Matter in West Africa. In France, the activist Assa Traoré was catapulted into fame as a result of the death of her brother, Adama Traoré, at the hands of police in 2016. When asked about her role in the struggle against police brutality in France, Traoré explained later, "We are fighting for our brother in the US, George Floyd, and for Adama," identifying the fight against anti-Blackness as a transnational and global movement.[30]

Today's BLM activists have a more inclusive and expansive view of freedom that is shored up by action. They "understand the need for action—direct self-transforming and structure-transforming action."[31] It is remarkable that, even in the 1960s, King understood that action must be "self-transforming" and "structure-transforming." Both approaches call for people to look inwardly and seek to transform themselves in order to transform the systems and the structures that they inhabit. Indeed, the need for an ethic that is inward and outward has also been noted by Black feminists like the writer Toni Cade Bambara, who wrote that "revolution begins with the self, in the self. We'd better take the time to fashion revolutionary selves, revolutionary lives, revolutionary relationships."[32] In other words, freedom movements should be self-reflective. The same sentiment emerges when you read the autobiographical works of Alicia Garza and Patrisse Cullors, both of whom explain a personal trajectory of justice work that connects to the larger movement.

---

[29]King, *Trumpet of Conscience*, 50.

[30]Lauren Collins, "Assa Traoré and the Fight for Black Lives in France," *New Yorker*, June 18, 2020.

[31]King, *Trumpet of Conscience*, 41.

[32]Toni Cade Bambara, "On the Issue of Roles," in *The Black Woman: An Anthology*, ed. Toni Cade Bambara (New York: Washington Square Press, 2005), 110.

The Language of the Unheard

Commenting on the uprising of 2020, civil rights activist and former member of SNCC Joyce Ladner noted how the legacy of the civil rights movement manifests today in Black Lives Matter. She also lamented the misappropriation of King's vision and how he is (mis)remembered: "I am angry when I read the blowback on Twitter against Martin Luther King III, who quoted his father as saying that 'a riot is the language of the unheard.'"[33] Ladner bemoans how King's memory is not only forgotten but flagrantly obviated. Twitter respondents told King that he did not understand the meaning of his own father's words because, in their view, Martin Luther King Jr. was nonviolent and always turned the other cheek. They conveniently ignored the fact that Dr. King spoke out often about the right to protest and to go to jail for what he called just causes. As King's daughter, Bernice King, wrote on Twitter, "Don't act like everyone loved my father. He was assassinated. Many who quote him now and evoke him to deter justice today would likely hate, and may already hate, the authentic King."[34] King's and Ladner's words are both crucial reminders that, in the twenty-first century, we have moved exceedingly far away from the reality of who King was. Restricting King to a box not only denies the radical parts of his vision, it has also become a way to silence contemporary activists and youth fighting for social action through movements like Black Lives Matter. A fuller understanding and deeper appreciation of Martin Luther King's entire philosophy makes clear that the actions and the ethos of Black Lives Matter are not far removed from King's legacy. What Ladner refers to here is the use of King's memory, image, and message for purposes that are not concerned with the total liberation of Black people. It is now possible to espouse views of King without actually caring about the freedom of Black people.[35]

---

[33] Joyce Ladner, "George Floyd's Killing Stirs Old Pain, Anger for a 1960s Activist," *Washington Post*, June 17, 2020.

[34] Ladner, "George Floyd's Killing."

[35] Dyson addresses a similar phenomenon in *I May Not Get There with You*, in

Furthermore, in a society where the celebration of MLK Day is a mere opportunity to share choice quotations and snippets from his most well-known speeches, there is little room for meaningful and sustained engagement with his greater vision.

Like Ladner, I want people to stop saying that Martin Luther King was against protest. This is so far from the truth, because he encourages people to find ways to protest:. "Every man of humane convictions must decide on the protest that best suits his convictions, but we must all protest."[36] King encouraged all forms of protest. He simply knew that nonviolence was the kind of movement to which God was calling him. Those eager to claim that King would disapprove of the Black Lives Matter protests in general, and the 2020 uprising specifically, ignore the radical King.

To be clear, Black people protesting the violation of their rights is a long-standing tradition in the United States and beyond. Just as the killing of Black people did not begin in the twenty-first century, protesting in defense of Black life did not begin with Black Lives Matter, nor even the civil rights movement. The movement to defend and uphold the humanity and dignity of Black people began as early as when the first group of enslaved Africans were forced here in 1619 and created their own ways to resist. Martin Luther King was not only in favor of protest, he encouraged everyone to participate in it. When King famously stated that "riot is the language of the unheard," he demonstrated his empathy for people who felt that they had no choice in their protest.

As a movement, Black Lives Matter is also unique in its collective approach to leadership. Eschewing the leadership approach that is based on a single leader, BLM has always been focused on the collective rather than exalting a single strong leader. It espouses a "grassroots, group-centered approach to leadership very much akin to the teachings of Black Freedom Movement icon Ella Baker."[37]

---

which he describes how King's words are being used against him in service of a conservative agenda.

[36]King, *Trumpet of Conscience*, 32.

[37]Ransby, *Making All Black Lives Matter*, 3.

Patrisse Cullors, Opal Tometi, and Alicia Garza were inspired to begin a movement of collective agitation that addressed anti-Black violence by the state and vigilantes. Recalling Audre Lorde's point that "there is no such thing as a single-issue struggle because we do not live single-issue lives," we are reminded that BLM cannot exist in a vacuum.[38] The stated mission of the BLM movement is to "eradicate white supremacy and build local power to intervene in state and local violence by vigilantes."[39] This far-reaching goal is imaginative. While the movement began in 2013, after the murder of George Floyd by police in 2020, it was propelled forward with new momentum. The viral video recorded by Darnella Frazier captured police officer Derek Chauvin kneeling on Floyd's neck for almost nine minutes. This generation of activists is not as different from Martin Luther King as their critics would have us believe. Like King, they understand the importance of global attention to their cause. They recall a statement that King made in 1965: "We won because we made the whole world pay attention to us."[40] Indeed, the recent nomination of Black Lives Matter to be recipients of the Nobel Peace Prize attests to the fact that the whole world is paying attention.

A New Movement of Youth and Social Action

My readings of *The Trumpet of Conscience* suggest that King would have certainly aligned himself with today's BLM activists. In "Youth and Social Action," King painstakingly describes and analyzes the young people of the civil rights generation, poring over what motivates them and how they respond to their quotidian injustice. King clearly has an affinity for them, is inspired by them, and finds them perplexing all at once. He is disturbed and moved by what he calls their "alienation." He approaches their cause with critique and empathy, grace and truth. He does not shy away from

---

[38]Audre Lorde, *Sister Outsider: Essays and Speeches*, rev. ed. (New York: Ten Speed Press, 2007), 138.

[39]See https://blacklivesmatter.com.

[40]Harding, *Martin Luther King*, 10.

critiquing them, but he also demonstrates care for their predicament.

King's reflections and evaluations about young people reveal his apparent heart for them. He was deeply concerned about their malaise and what he called their alienation. In his view, that alienation was "rampant" among young people especially.[41] It would serve us well to be reminded that one of the most impactful civil rights organizations was formed as a result of these feelings that King and the other leaders at the vanguard of the movement voiced regarding young people. The Student Nonviolent Coordinating Committee emerged in 1960 as the youth wing of the Southern Christian Leadership Conference. The idea for the movement came from Ella Baker, when she "invited herself" to a meeting held by a group of students at Shaw University and encouraged them to maintain their autonomy in relation to the SCLC.[42] According to archival materials in the King papers collection, he called on the students to form "some type of continuing organization" and "to delve deeper into the philosophy of nonviolence."[43] SNCC was responsible for coordinating students in Freedom Rides from May to December 1961, a form of direct action in response to the 1960 Supreme Court ruling in *Boynton v. Virginia* that segregation of interstate transportation facilities, including bus terminals, was unconstitutional.

As the Trayvon Generation, today's youth activists espouse a range of politics informed by their coming to age in an unprecedented time. "These are unprecedented attitudes because this generation was born and matured in unprecedented conditions."[44] Rarely a year goes by that my college students are not rocked by the death of an unarmed Black person at the hands of police. "Their radicalism is growing because the power structure of today

---

[41]"Alienation is not confined to young people, but it is rampant among them" (King, *Trumpet of Conscience*, 44).

[42]Ransby, *Ella Baker,* 242.

[43]"Student Nonviolent Coordinating Committee (SNCC)," April 15, 1960, to May 1, 1971, https://kinginstitute.stanford.edu.

[44]King, *Trumpet of Conscience*, 38.

is unrelenting in defending not only its social system but the evils it contains; so, naturally, it is intensifying the opposition."[45] Just as they were during King's day, today's youth are trying "to give better expression to their own world"—something for which we must applaud rather than chide them. In their effort to give better expression to the world, today's young activists look for new vocabularies to express their rage and propel forward their vision of a new world. Their example is spiritually inspiring because they bring the anger and the passion of Jesus to their fight. They are unabashed in their willingness to speak truth to power and do not shrink back in their zeal as they imagine this better world.

How would King speak to today's youth? How would he address the young activists at the forefront of the Black Lives Matter movement? Had he lived to an old age and known he was going to die, would he, like John Lewis, have penned an editorial to be published after his funeral? Might his message have been similar to John Lewis's words in July 2020? Would it sing with admiration and inspiration as we find in Lewis's words?

> While my time here has now come to an end, I want you to know that in the last days and hours of my life you inspired me. You filled me with hope about the next chapter of the great American story when you used your power to make a difference in our society. Millions of people motivated simply by human compassion laid down the burdens of division. Around the country and the world you set aside race, class, age, language and nationality to demand respect for human dignity.[46]

Here, Lewis speaks directly to the BLM generation and draws comparisons between the most recent victims of anti-Black violence and those he witnessed during his youth. He writes,

---

[45]King, *Trumpet of Conscience*, 41–42.

[46]John Lewis, "Together, You Can Redeem the Soul of Our Nation," *New York Times*, July 30, 2020.

Emmett Till was my George Floyd. He was my Rayshard Brooks, Sandra Bland and Breonna Taylor. He was 14 when he was killed, and I was only 15 years old at the time. I will never ever forget the moment when it became so clear that he could easily have been me. In those days, fear constrained us like an imaginary prison, and troubling thoughts of potential brutality committed for no understandable reason were the bars.[47]

A Radical Reimagining

Reading King's thoughts about the youth of his generation, I am compelled by his references to their creativity, which also extends to so many of the activists I encounter today. "It is difficult to exaggerate the creative contribution of young [people]."[48] It is thrilling to see the creative work of young people who are currently advancing justice. They are pushing the generation ahead of them not only to imagine but to create a more just world. Even when we disagree with some of the tools they use, like the creation of "cancel culture," their creativity and innovation are unequivocal. People like Darnella Frazier, who filmed the murder of George Floyd on her cellphone and then circulated it on social media are creative and action-oriented. They are like the students who took our "Where #BlackLivesMatter Meets #MeToo" class in 2018 and created a moving documentary, *Am I Next?*, in which they combined and presented in creative ways original work with statistics about anti-Black violence. They are the ones whom Elizabeth Alexander referred to as the Trayvon Generation—the young people inspired, nourished, and nurtured by the Black Lives Matter movement.[49] Their ongoing exposure to anti-Black racism has inspired them to social action. Today's youth dedicated to Black Lives Matter seem to have some of the same commitments as King when he wrote the lectures that form *The Trumpet of Conscience*. They are asking that the United States face

[47]Lewis, "Together."
[48]King, *Trumpet of Conscience*, 46.
[49]Elizabeth Alexander, "The Trayvon Generation," *New Yorker*, June 15, 2020.

its interrelated flaws—racism, poverty, militarism, and materialism. Like the Black freedom movement King led, today the Black Lives Matter movement is "exposing the evils that are rooted deeply in the whole structure of our society. It reveals systemic rather than superficial flaws and suggests that radical reconstruction of society itself is the real issue to be faced."[50] The gutting of the system is nothing if not a radical reimagining.

There are, nonetheless, stark differences between the young people described in "Youth and Social Action" and today's activists. Unlike the young people with whom King interacted during his life, we cannot say of this generation that "they are in serious revolt against old values and have not yet concretely formulated new ones,"[51] because this generation is strategic in its organizing. They have dreamed of, imagined, and established new plans. In fact, their plans are concrete, explicit, well thought out, and well established. They "plot, plan, strategize, and mobilize."[52] They propose concrete solutions to the social injustice they are witnessing.[53] They understand the importance of the strategic work necessary to accompany their activism and to ensure its longevity. Similarly, in my years as a professor, I have seen how my undergraduate students who are working toward racial justice make demands of the administration to bring impactful and meaningful change. Among the lessons that we learn from *The Trumpet of Conscience* is that we cannot dismiss today's young people nor overlook their contributions. We should appreciate their leadership, for we desperately need it. We need their voices, their visions, their collaboration, their activism, and their votes. The movement to end racial injustice will be incomplete without them. The urgency is real. Black lives are on the line.

---

[50]King, *Trumpet of Conscience*, 40.

[51]King, *Trumpet of Conscience*, 40.

[52]Killer Mike, "Rapper Killer Mike Speech Transcript during Atlanta Protests," rev.com (blog), May 30, 2020, www.rev.com/blog.

[53]One example of this is Project Zero, the nonprofit organization that came out of the Ferguson uprising.

A REVOLUTION OF LOVE AND CREATIVITY

The time is short today, just as King said it was in the 1960s: "But we do not have much time. The revolutionary spirit is already world-wide. If the anger of the peoples of the world at the injustice of things is to be channeled into a revolution of love and creativity, we must begin now to work, urgently, with all peoples, to shape a new world."[54] What he describes in this passage takes on a different yet still meaningful implication today. We must remain vigilant in the face of injustice and create possibilities for fighting against it that are inclusive of different communities. It has become common in 2020 to circulate booklists that advance the call to antiracism. There are books to educate people about the lives, experiences, and history of Black people in this country—books aimed at white people to help them unlearn racism and to grapple with their difficulties in discussing racism. There are also books for children and young adults, as well as those aimed at teachers to encourage them to diversify their curriculum. These books are treated as solutions that are going to teach us to be antiracist, to equip our churches to be antiracist, to create schools that are antiracist, and to embrace antiracism as a way of life—all necessary in a society for change to happen.

The efforts that some white people are making to educate themselves about racism is important, but I fear that this learning is allowing people to applaud themselves just for their efforts. I am not convinced that the people I know doing all of this reading are also aware that action and policy are just as, if not more, important as their consciousness raising. The work of abolition requires a coupling of education and action. King was obsessed with the problem of how to effect lasting and meaningful change. Reading books is not the end goal, but rather a starting point or a pit stop on

---

[54]King, *Trumpet of Conscience*, 51.

the way to a just society. Sociologist Saida Grundy made a similar point: "Raising awareness about racism is not a means in itself of correcting injustice."[55]

Black Lives Matter is one of the largest movements in the world. But so much work remains to be done to adopt antiracist policies, to realize antiracist education, to amplify and elevate the voices of Black people, to eliminate the harm caused by anti-Blackness, and to demonstrate that all Black lives do matter. The Good Samaritan analogy that King made in his "I've Been to the Mountaintop" speech invites us to suffer with those who are suffering and to act on their behalf. If we are to do the work of justice alongside others, we will have to give up *something*. Justice work comes at a cost. For me as a Black woman with class and heterosexual privilege, the cost may involve changing how I speak to my children about these topics. Today, my four-year-old marches around the house saying, "Black Lives Matter." I hope that, by the time she is in college, she understands enough to tell the people who say, "All lives matter," why we say "Black lives matter," but also that she does not *have to* because Black lives will not be under attack as they are today.

Structural Change

The roots are in the system. In our class discussions with students about systemic racism, my co-teacher, friend, and colleague Shawn McGuffey cautions our students, "We are all swimming in the same dirty water." Shawn learned this expression from his mother, who was born and raised in Kentucky during the 1950s. She means here that racism is the air we breathe. All people in the United States are affected by anti-Black racism. Black people suffer and are also implicated by it. It is a system that cannot be undone without inter-rogation and action. Interrogation alone is not enough; it must be coupled with action. In *The Trumpet of Conscience*, when King

---

[55]Saida Grundy, "The False Promise of Anti-Racism Books," *The Atlantic*, July 21, 2020.

describes the three different kinds of young people in the 1960s, he identifies one factor that united them: "All of them agree that only by structural change can current evils be eliminated, because the roots are in the system rather than in men or in faulty operation." King continues, "Their rebelliousness comes from having been frustrated in seeking change within the framework of the existing society"[56]—a point that is also true of young people today. The extreme popularity of socialist candidate Bernie Sanders among young people speaks to this frustration. It is not that the system is broken and they want to fix it; they want an entirely new system that will allow them to rebuild from the ground up. Contrary to what some like to believe about Martin Luther King, he was not entirely opposed to socialism. Inherent to King's critique of capitalism as a system that failed the poor majority with whom he continuously aligned himself is an implicit embrace of socialism.[57]

The Black Lives Matter movement shows us how little has changed since King wrote the lectures in *The Trumpet of Conscience*, especially regarding government inaction around racial injustice. "Congress is horrified not by the conditions of Negro life but at the product of these conditions—the Negro himself."[58] This remains true today. Many of our politicians are more concerned about what inequality is producing in people than the fact that inequality exists. Similarly, people are more concerned about being called "racist" than they are about eliminating racism.

I had a close-up view of this dynamic in my own town when an African American teacher at the middle school was placed on administrative leave after teaching a lesson about racism during her sixth-grade English class. She said, "Ahmaud Arbery was killed by racist white people, and many cops are racist." When I asked my own twelve-year-old son how he felt about the statement, he said that "most cops are racist" would have been more accurate. The

---

[56]King, *Trumpet of Conscience*, 40.

[57]Matthew Miles Goodrich, "The Forgotten Socialist History of Martin Luther King Jr.," inthesetimes.com, January 15, 2018.

[58]King, *Trumpet of Conscience*, 17.

reality of racism in policing is one that Black people live with every day. By placing the teacher on leave, the district administration sent a dangerous message to students and teachers that racism should not be discussed and that being called "racist" is worse than racism itself. This is one of the problems of our society: we care more about *words* than about *systems*. That dynamic emanates from the same place when we commemorate King by focusing more on his words than his actions.

Today, I continue to be troubled that people forget about Martin Luther King's commitment to economic justice and his critique of class hierarchies—and that those class and racial divisions fragmenting our society have only become more entrenched. After all, when King wrote, "It is precisely when young [Black people] threw off their middle-class values that they made an historic social contribution," it was a clear indictment of how the respectability politics of the middle class were leading to widespread complacency.[59] When he focused on economic injustice, King was demonstrating an understanding of how intersectionality works, even before that term was used. Today, the Black Lives Matter movement invites us to question how far we have come since the civil rights movement of the 1950s and 1960s—and since the arrival of the first Black people in 1619 and the subsequent centuries of enslavement that continue to stain this country. Indeed, Black Lives Matter is a movement that is elevating conversations about race and racism as well as advancing justice in the United States. As such, it is reminiscent of what King was talking about when he said that "the Negro freedom movement . . . elevated the moral level of the nation."[60] If, indeed, a moral reckoning is taking place today, it is because of the Black Lives Matter movement.

But how widespread is this conviction? As King suggests, "Listen to the argument for peace, not as a dream, but as a practical possibility: something to choose and use."[61] Referencing the language

---

[59]King, *Trumpet of Conscience*, 47.

[60]King, *Trumpet of Conscience*, 48.

[61]King, *Trumpet of Conscience*, 43.

of dreams, King dislodges it here from the imagination and urges us to see it as a possibility, as a reality that is not so far away. Not only was King in favor of any form of protest, he spoke cogently in defense of protesters who did not use nonviolence as their primary modus operandi. He explained why people in impoverished urban neighborhoods were okay with damaging property: "Why were they so violent with property then? Because property represents the white power structure, which they were attacking and trying to destroy."[62]

King's explanation of this dynamic reminds me of a widely circulated video of activist Kimberly Jones called *How Can We Win?* Jones's speech became popular in 2020 during that summer's uprising. I doubt that people would compare the two speakers, but I do so here because we can learn from such a comparison. Jones asks us, "Why are people so broke, so food insecure, so poor . . . that their only shot to get what they need is steal?" She explains that the origins of Black people in the United States is fundamentally yoked to economics, because Black people have had everything taken from them. Using the analogy of a monopoly game, Jones notes that for more than four hundred years, Black people have not only had to work for free but were forced to work on behalf of other people. She explains that, "For 400 rounds of Monopoly without the resources and then for fifty years . . . Why do you burn down your community? It's not ours, we don't own anything! For four hundred years we built your wealth, then when we built our wealth you came in and slaughtered us, and burned our neighborhoods to the ground," she says, referring to Tulsa and Rosewood.[63] Her explanation recalls the description of intercommunal violence by Huey Newton of the Black Panther Party for Self-Defense: "It is a problem that at its root is an uneven distribution of resources and power and a very human—if still distressing and painful—response to not having what you need to live well."[64] Jones's impassioned

---

[62]King, *Trumpet of Conscience*, 59.

[63]Kimberly Jones, *How Can We Win?*, David Jones Media, YouTube video, 6:46 mins., https://www.youtube.com/watch?v=llci8MVh8J4.

[64]Garza, *Purpose of Power*, 115.

speech is a far cry from the sermons that King preached and which touch on essential points about economic injustice and four hundred years of struggle and pain. The video came about because of a documentary that she was working on after talking to people who had been protesting, when it became clear to her that the protesters knew that the narrative focus was going to be on looting. Her nearly seven-minute speech resulted from her conversations with people, who had participated in the uprising on the streets of Atlanta. She ends by saying, "People should be grateful that Black people want justice, not revenge."

Kimberly Jones's stirring speech makes several relevant points. First, she names the racial fatigue that comes with centuries of being put behind as a result of slavery. Second, she connects the uprising to the systemic racism that has routinely crippled Black people's ability to succeed and get ahead. She also goes into detail about slavery as an economic system linked to the wealth and success of the United States. In this brief video, Jones distills with clarity and precision the reality of racism as an intractable force that shapes the lives of Black people in the United States. Economic and racial inequality walk hand in hand down the corridor of injustice. "And it is getting worse, as the gap between the poor and 'affluent society' increases."[65] It is even worse today than when King wrote those words several decades ago, because the chasm between the rich and the poor is widening into an enormous gulf where the rich get increasingly richer and the poor get still poorer.

Love and Action

After Boston College launched the first-ever Forum on Racial Justice in the fall of 2020, I was invited to participate on a panel about formation and justice in higher education. I shared that when I reflect on formation, love is what first comes to mind. There can be no formation and no justice without attention to love. The impera-

---

[65]King, *Trumpet of Conscience*, 57.

tive to be attentive, reflective, and loving as the pillars of formative education fit seamlessly with Black Lives Matter. I have seen this in my work inside and outside the classroom.

In summer 2019 I taught a course in Paris to a group of thirteen students, most of whom had already taken the "Where #BlackLives-Matter Meets #MeToo" course. This class was titled "Paris Noir: The Literature and Culture of Black Paris." We examined the Négritude movement begun by a group of Black immigrant students educated in France during the 1930s and explored theories of race and racism by canonical thinkers like Frantz Fanon. We read novels by authors including Gisèle Pineau from Guadeloupe and Fatou Diome, who was born in Senégal and migrated to France at the age of eighteen. We viewed documentaries such as *Ouvrir la voix* by Amandine Gay, who chronicles how racism and sexism affect Black French women. We had an awe-inspiring roster of class speakers, including the well-known Afro-French journalist Rokhaya Diallo, who now writes for the *Washington Post*. Our final speaker was Assa Traoré, a child of Malian immigrants and an activist who has been at the helm of the Black Lives Matter movement in France since her brother Adama Traoré was killed by police in 2016. When my students learned about the Black Lives Matter movement in France, their eyes were opened to the global reverberations of anti-Blackness. Many of them had participated in and led demonstrations on campus themselves. Because they had studied the history and literature, they were able to locate the Black Lives Matter movement in Paris within a broader context of anti-Black racism that French intellectuals, writers, and artists have been documenting for decades. I wanted my students to think critically about Black Lives Matter as a global movement, to understand that anti-Blackness was not only a problem for the United States, and to situate the movement within a larger Black studies intellectual project.

Assa Traoré's visit to our class was especially powerful because she laid out a strategic plan for social justice organizing. "Il ne faut pas rester à sa place, il faut s'imposer" (You must not stay in your place, you must assert yourselves and act), she kept repeating. Her visit occurred during the last week of class, and with her inspiration, we ended our time together in Paris on an incredibly high note. But the joy of that high note threatened to dissipate a few nights later when my students were out at a nightclub and witnessed a scene of police brutality. They watched in horror as French police grabbed a Black man, handled him brutally, and shoved him into the car. Walking home from the scene, a few of the students who were Muslim prayed together for the safety of the brother they saw being taken away. They wondered if he, like Adama Traoré and so many other Black French men, would die in police custody. They were traumatized. The following morning, we gathered to reflect on what they witnessed. My students were visibly upset and agitated. They felt helpless and enraged. Among the things that bothered them most was that other people in the crowd outside the nightclub did not seem to even pay attention to what was going on. My students were attentive to what was happening, knowing that police brutality was an insidious reality in Paris.

This anecdote demonstrates that in affirming that Black lives matter, justice and formative education can intersect. If we are to teach students to be attentive, reflective, and loving, then we must confront injustice and not turn away from incidents of pain and suffering. It requires that we acknowledge the hurt and harm caused by institutions, even—perhaps especially—those we hold in high esteem. I had to encourage my students to explore their pain and the harm they witnessed, and to process what it felt like to witness such an egregious disregard for Black life. To be clear, the goal was not to have them move past it but to work through it and try to figure out what healing and justice might look like in the context of what they just witnessed. The students demonstrated not only an ability to analyze what happened in relation to a history of anti-Black racism, but also a desire to be attentive in a way that leads to action. Their desire for justice motivated them to think about the next steps and actions. The great Black feminist writer Toni Cade Bambara wrote that "the job of the writer is to make revolution irresistible." In my view, the job of the formative educator is to make justice irresistible.

Martin Luther King preached, taught, and lived justice. He led with love and action, constantly calling attention to the fact that justice *is* what love looks like in public. In *A Testament of Hope*, King writes, "I am not sad that black Americans are rebelling; this was not only inevitable, but eminently desirable. Without this magnificent ferment among Negroes, the old evasions and procrastinations would have continued indefinitely."[66] This point is just as persuasive and applicable today as it was over fifty years ago. When we encounter those who are leading and protesting along with the Black Lives Matter movement, this is what we remember, and what *The Trumpet of Conscience* asks us to consider: if we do not stand for this movement with racial justice and antiracism at the center, how can we claim to believe in a common humanity?

---

[66]Martin Luther King Jr., *A Testament of Hope: The Essential Writings and Speeches*, ed. James M. Washington (1986; repr. New York: HarperCollins, 2003).

3

Ending Sexual Violence

*If we do not help the rape survivors what will happen
to them?*

On the second day of Christine Blasey Ford's testimony before
the US Senate Judiciary Committee in 2018, I could not stop crying. I wept intermittently throughout the day for reasons related to
Blasey Ford and beyond. Ford testified to address her allegations
that Brett Kavanaugh had sexually assaulted her almost forty years
prior. As a Black feminist scholar and activist, the hearings were
painfully reminiscent of the Supreme Court nomination hearings of
the 1990s when Anita Hill testified about her allegations of sexual
harassment at the hands of Clarence Thomas.

On the second day of Blasey Ford's testimony, I was traveling
from Boston to Chicago for the twentieth-anniversary celebration
of the performance *Story of a Rape Survivor*. After boarding the
plane, I accidentally put my coffee on the wrong seat while placing my luggage in the overhead compartment. The coffee spilled.
When I returned to what I thought was my seat, a white man was
waiting for me and furiously started to shout at me for what I had
done to his seat. I tried to explain that I thought the seat was mine
and that it was an accident. He continued to shout, calling me stupid.
I asked him not to raise his voice. Eventually the flight attendant

intervened, I went to my seat, and the women around me looked on sympathetically. I could not stop crying.

When the flight landed in Chicago, I saw reports of Dr. Blasey Ford on the screen and began to cry again. "I am not here today because I want to be. I am terrified," Dr. Blasey Ford said. The terror was audible in her voice, which seemed to tremble with her every word. I was crying for her and for all the survivors I know. I was crying for those who shared their stories in public and for those who never would. I know from the work that I have done with survivors and my research on rape culture that coming forward to share their stories of sexual violence is already challenging without the pressure of a national (and largely unsympathetic) audience let alone being televised. I was crying over my sadness at the small and large injustices that occur every day and that train women to believe that we do not matter as much as men. I was crying because I remember being in eighth grade when Anita Hill testified before the Senate Judiciary Committee before Clarence Thomas was appointed to the Supreme Court. I was crying because I know too many women who do not feel that their voices, their stories, their trauma . . . their lives matter. If we really believe that—in the words of King—"injustice anywhere is indeed a threat to justice everywhere," then the forms of injustice that are gender specific should be the concern of anyone who cares about justice.[1] Taking these words seriously means including sexism, misogyny, transphobia, and homophobia in our march to freedom. Although King is hardly known for waging a struggle against sexism and misogyny, any accurate application of his message requires attention to the ways in which sexism, misogyny, patriarchy, and gender inequality are also concerns of a faith that does justice. Many of his positions in *The Trumpet of Conscience* can be applied to the movement for gender equality in general, and most recently, the Me Too movement in particular.

A better model who explicitly championed the rights of women

---

[1] King, "Letter from a Birmingham Jail" ("For years now I have heard the words 'Wait!' It rings in the ear of every Negro with a piercing familiarity").

as she participated in the Black freedom movement was Fannie Lou Hamer, a civil rights and voting rights activist who is not nearly as well known as King. When Hamer famously declared that "nobody's free until everybody's free," it was not only in reference to race. "Everybody" means any human being, regardless of gender, sexuality, age, and ability. Our freedom relies on and depends on the liberation of others. Individual freedom matters little without attention to the collective. Lesbian poet Audre Lorde unpacks this point even more, explaining, "I am not free as long as any woman is unfree, even when her shackles are very different from my own. And I am not free as long as one person of Color remains chained. Nor is any one of you."[2] Our freedoms are linked. If we are to dream the revolutionary dreams that Nikki Giovanni alludes to in her poem referenced earlier, we must advocate for people who are different from us. Although King often mentioned the poor, marginalized, and vulnerable, he rarely, if ever, mentioned women. Central to King's philosophy was the idea that the struggle against injustice must include people beyond those it victimized. In other words, non-Black people need to work alongside Black people in the fight against racism. Wealthy people need to join in the fight against social inequality and poverty. People of all genders must be engaged in the fight against sexist discrimination and gender-based violence. Despite King's failure to address gender injustice and inequality between men and women, his philosophy suggests that we should pay attention to every form of injustice, including the oppressions faced by women. When we read *The Trumpet of Conscience* carefully, signs of this thinking are clear throughout.

"BUT SOME OF US ARE BRAVE"

Unfortunately, in the 1960s, Martin Luther King was not alone in excluding women from the purview of his activism for racial

---

[2]Lorde, *Sister Outsider,* 132–33.

justice. In the twenty-first century, we see that, despite the inclusive origins of the Black Lives Matter movement, Black women and girls are often forgotten in the cause. Today the astonishing gender gap in mobilizing against racial violence is being addressed by activists like Kimberlé Crenshaw, Aishah Shahidah Simmons, and Tarana Burke. Although Black women activists have been at the forefront of centering Black women and girls in the struggle against gender-based violence, they are rarely the subjects of this activism. The movement is widely perceived as being exclusively for and about white women. Activists working at the intersection of racial and gender justice today walk in the footsteps of women organizers, activists, and scholars who have been calling attention to how multiple oppressions operate in the lives of Black women. This dynamic recalls the title of one of the founding academic works of Black feminist thinking: *All the Women Are White, All the Blacks Are Men, But Some of Us Are Brave: Black Women's Studies*.[3] Published in 1982, this canonical anthology was part of a surge of writing by Black feminists within and outside the academy. In this time of intense productivity and activity, a number of novels, anthologies, and other creative works were published as well.[4] Featuring the work of scholars such as Mary Helen Washington, creative writers such as Alice Walker, and cultural critics such as Michelle Wallace, the book registered the multifaceted contributions of Black feminist thought. It transformed women's studies by establishing Black feminist studies as a generative field of theory and praxis. Almost forty years after the publication of the collection, it is worth noting that

---

[3]Patricia Bell Scott, Gloria T. Hull, and Barbara Smith, eds., *All the Women Are White, All the Blacks Are Men, But Some of Us Are Brave: Black Women's Studies* (New York: Feminist Press at CUNY, 1982).

[4]If, as Hull, Smith, and Scott passionately state in the introduction, "Black women studies must consider as primary the knowledge that will save Black women's lives" (xxv), then even celebrity survivor narratives can be important sites of analysis for understanding why and how the lives of Black women come to matter within popular culture. Today, Black women like Gabrielle Union, Tarana Burke, and Salamishah Tillet carry on this Black feminist legacy by identifying ways that Black women survivors continue to be marginalized within the antiviolence movement.

the provocative title continues to resonate as we observe how often in the media Black women's labor, voices, activism, pain, creative genius, and experiences are erased. In the anthology, the authors call for a radical approach to the study of "supposedly 'ordinary' Black women whose 'unexceptional' actions enabled us and the race to survive."[5] The same is true today of the Me Too movement, which is largely considered a white women's movement, despite its origins in the activism of Tarana Burke.

As noted regarding the Black Lives Matter movement, the struggle was inspired by the death of Black men and boys but initiated by Black queer women activists. This illustrates how often Black women will put their bodies on the line to protest against injustices meted against Black men, although when injustice is inflicted upon Black women, we are rarely supported by the same level of outrage. The labor of Black women has always propelled the movement against racial justice, even when others seek to render them invisible. When Ida B. Wells began her antilynching campaign, she also lambasted the frequency of sexual violence against Black women and girls. In a speech delivered in 1895 Wells declared, "The rape of helpless Negro girls, which began in slavery days, still continues without reproof from church, state, or press."[6] Wells, known for her journalism and antilynching crusading also paid attention to how racial violence was inflicted upon Black women.

In 2014, when Kimberlé Crenshaw initiated the movement that became #SayHerName to demonstrate how Black women are victimized by police violence, she did so with the same intention. She saw how infrequently those Black women who were killed by police were placed at the center of collective organizing against state and police violence. The #SayHerName campaign amplifies this problem:

Black women and girls as young as 7 and as old as 93 have been killed by the police, though we rarely hear their names.

---

[5]Scott et al., *All the Women Are White*, 233.
[6]Cited in Danielle L. McGuire, *The Dark End of the Street* (New York: Vintage, 2010), xviii.

Knowing their names is a necessary but not a sufficient condition for lifting up their stories which in turn provides a much clearer view of the wide-ranging circumstances that make Black women's bodies disproportionately subject to police violence. To lift up their stories, and illuminate police violence against Black women, we need to know who they are, how they lived, and why they suffered at the hands of police.[7]

As part of the campaign, a report was written to elaborate on the statistics of how police violence affects women. Written by the scholar Andrea Ritchie, the report explains how Black women and girls are often left out of organizing around Black Lives Matter. "Say Her Name sheds light on Black women's experiences of police violence in an effort to support a gender inclusive approach to racial justice that centers all Black lives equally."[8]

Despite the efforts of Say Her Name, in 2020 we once again saw how racial justice is not gender-inclusive when the outrage around the death of George Floyd and Ahmaud Arbery eclipsed the police killing of Breonna Taylor. To be clear, it is not that the women who began Black Lives Matter were not inclusive in their approach, it was that the most public outcry and mobilization in protest against Black deaths foregrounded Black men and boys: Trayvon Martin, Michael Brown, Tamir Rice, Eric Garner, Philando Castile, Ahmaud Arbery, and George Floyd. The names of Black men and boys killed by police have become nationally recognized. But are we as familiar with Rekia Boyd, Eleanor Bumpers, Jessica Hampton, and Aiyana Stanley-Jones? Although Sandra Bland and Breonna Taylor have risen to prominence, they represent rare exceptions rather than the norm. No vision for racial justice is complete without an intersectional perspective. As artist and activist Scheherazade Tillet notes, for too many Black women and girls, "there is a grief to knowing

---

[7]See African American Policy Forum, https://aapf.org/sayhername.

[8]African American Policy Forum, *Say Her Name Report*, July 2015, https://44bbdc6e-01a4-4a9a-88bc-731c6524888e.filesusr.com/ugd/62e126_9223ee35c2694ac3bd3f2171504ca3f7.pdf, 2.

that your stories will not be central to the movement."[9] When the stories of Black women and girls are erased, the vision for racial justice is incomplete.

One of the most blatant examples of this erasure is the case of Oluatoyin "Toyin" Salau, a nineteen-year-old Black Lives Matter activist who was raped and killed in June 2020. In the maelstrom of anti-Black violence that unfolded throughout 2020 and absorbed much of the nation, this instance of a young Black woman's rape and murder barely registered in the media. Who will organize for Toyin, a Black Lives Matter activist? Who will remember her name and mobilize for her cause? The example confirms a confluence of racial violence and sexual violence that too many are slow to end. A widespread disregard for Black women's stories and pain is what prompted the beginnings of Say Her Name. Like Black Lives Matter, its invitation was a humble request to "say her name"—to acknowledge, honor, and remember the Black women who have been killed by police.

These examples also show us that Black women have always defended Black women, even when the same racial solidarity was not extended to them. Abbey Lincoln posed the question "Who will revere the Black woman?" at the end of an essay she wrote in 1966. "Who will keep our neighborhoods safe for Black innocent womanhood? Black womanhood is outraged and humiliated. Black womanhood cries for dignity and restitution and salvation. Black womanhood wants and needs protection, and keeping, and holding. Who will assuage her indignation? Who will keep her precious and pure? Who will glorify and proclaim her beautiful image? To whom will she cry rape?"[10]

These questions are necessary in a world that does not value

---

[9] Christen A. Johnson, "Black Girls and Women Are Often Left Out of the Social Justice Movement. These 2 Sisters Have Been Fighting to Change That," *Chicago Tribune*, June 19, 2020.

[10] Abbey Lincoln, "Who Will Revere the Black Woman?" Ebony.com, February 12, 2013, www.ebony.com. This essay appeared in the September 1966 issue of *Negro Digest*, John H. Johnson's first magazine. *Negro Digest* was founded in 1942 and renamed *Black World* in 1970. The magazine remained in print until 1976.

Black women equally. While the celebrity iteration of #MeToo can be critiqued for how it primarily amplified the voices of affluent and famous white women at the expense of Black and Brown women, what the movement signaled—or at the very least invited—was a culture shift in how we respond to various forms of gender-based violence ranging from sexual harassment and street harassment to rape and domestic violence. It called attention to the tacit and overt acceptance of violence against women and girls in our society. Still, the focus within the Me Too movement was overwhelmingly white and privileged. Actor Gabrielle Union expressed a similar sentiment when she told the *New York Times,* "I think the floodgates have opened for white women. . . . I don't think it's a coincidence whose pain has been taken seriously. Whose pain we have shown historically and continued to show. Whose pain is tolerable and whose pain is intolerable. And whose pain needs to be addressed now."[11] Her point is well taken because, often when the term "reckoning" is used, it fails to account for whom the reckoning is happening. Union's critique rightly calls out how the coverage of #MeToo has primarily centered on the survivor narratives, testimonies, and activism of white women.

What does it mean to stand with survivors? What does it look like to believe survivors? How can we enact a justice that advances a vision of the world without sexual violence? Taking seriously the question that introduces this chapter—*If we do not stand with the survivors of sexual violence, what will become of them, and not what will become of us?*—means that we must pause to ask what the implications are for a world in which survivors are not believed. The unnoticed and unanswered question is, how do we imagine a world in which perpetrators are held accountable and survivors are not only believed but supported? My frame of reference for what this might look like is shaped by the work that I have done as an antirape academic, advocate, and activist.

---

[11]Haley Krischer, "We're Going to Need More Gabrielle Union," *New York Times,* December 5, 2017.

Throughout my twenties and thirties, I worked with A Long Walk Home, a nonprofit organization whose mission is to empower young artists and activists to end violence against all girls and women and to advocate for racial and gender equity in schools, communities, and the United States at large. A Long Walk Home has been especially impactful as an organization that empowers, inspires, and mobilizes young people to end violence against Black women and girls. A Long Walk Home evolved from being an intimate exchange between sisters to a student project, an organization, and into a movement as a result of the brave work of Salamishah and Scheherazade Tillet. The Tillet sisters began their work because Salamishah was the victim of sexual violence in college while she was a first-year student, as well as when she studied abroad her junior year. When she disclosed to her sister that she had been raped, Scheherazade, the younger sister, was determined to help Salamishah heal. As a student of social documentary, she used her camera to document her sister's journey from victim to survivor. At the urging of a college mentor, she turned what began as a photo exhibition into a multimedia arts performance about one individual woman's story to one that is performed by a group of women. The performance *Story of a Rape Survivor* (SOARS) includes dance, singing, and theatrical performance. Together, the women featured in the performance embody what Salamishah had experienced, using art to tell her story. It was a powerful example of art as an agent for social change and an instrument of healing from trauma.

Several years after the creation of SOARS, our first program, A Long Walk Home targeted a different audience. Aware of the alarming statistic that Black and Brown girls are three times more likely to experience gender-based violence (street harassment, sexual assault, teen-dating violence) than their white peers, we began the Girl/Friends program. Girl/Friends is a yearlong creative arts program that empowers teen girls to become antiviolence advocates in their schools and communities. These girls go on to be local social justice leaders, participating in a global movement to end violence against women and girls.

As a board member, performer, and lecturer for A Long Walk Home, I occupied many roles in the organization where I learned myriad skills for organizing against sexual violence and went through training at rape crisis centers in Boston and Washington, DC. I discovered what it meant to support survivors, beginning simply with believing their stories. I witnessed the power of youth-led organizing for community transformation. I became acquainted with the utility of art therapy in accessing and addressing sexual trauma. Starting and building a nonprofit organization also provided me with tangible skills in fundraising, organizing, and strategic visioning. But I also learned more abstract, invaluable lessons that informed and transformed my understanding of justice. I learned about the importance of walking hand in hand with survivors of sexual violence, and looking to them for leadership in the movement. I learned how to ask the question that King reframes in his retelling of the Good Samaritan parable: "If I do not stop for the rape survivors, what will happen to them?" From the moment I began performing in *Story of a Rape Survivor*, people I knew would approach me with their stories of sexual violence. From family members to friends whom I had known since high school, these survivors shared their experiences of sexual violence. Why hadn't they felt safe telling me before? Were they afraid of not being believed? Was there was too much silence surrounding the issue that they did not feel comfortable breaking it? How had I perpetuated those silences, either explicitly or implicitly? As more women began to disclose their experiences to me, it became clear that I needed more skills and knowledge. I undertook the forty-hour training at the Boston Area Rape Crisis Center (BARCC) to become a rape crisis counselor. The training included the issues of childhood sexual abuse, incest, and intimate partner violence. I also began to see and question the ways in which violence was present in my own childhood.

When people learn about the work I do in the antirape movement, they often assume that I am also a rape survivor. Their assumptions do not arise simply because people are aware of the statistic that one in three women will be raped in their lifetime, but because they observe my actions and cannot imagine any other reason I would care so much. Sometimes I poke through their assumptions to ask what rape means to them. I often explain my commitment to this work in terms that we use to talk about racial injustice or other forms of gender-based discrimination: rape is a human rights problem that concerns us all and that each of us must do our part to end. For these reasons, the movement to end gender-based violence must be included in the larger struggle against injustice.

"ALL LIFE IS INTERRELATED"

So what do the lectures that form *The Trumpet of Conscience* teach us about gender-based violence as a broader justice issue? In truth, painfully little in the historical record indicates that Martin Luther King cared about issues like sexual harassment, rape, and domestic violence. However, if we follow the evolution of his thinking in areas like economic injustice and the war in Vietnam, we can discern how he might have eventually intervened in this topic also. For example, in the final lecture, "A Christmas Sermon on Peace," King emphasizes the interrelatedness of society: "It really boils down to this: that all life is interrelated."[12]

The idea that all life is interrelated makes me think about intersectionality—the theory that explains how multiple oppressions influence identity. Intersectionality is a lens for understanding how oppression operates in society. It enables us to see people's experiences through a prism that accounts for the different ways that they are marginalized and oppressed. For example, a straight Black woman with class privilege faces different challenges from a gay Black woman who is socioeconomically disadvantaged. King took even further the view that everything is interrelated by suggesting that people who do not have marginalized identities are affected by the oppressions that plague others. "Whatever affects one directly,

---

[12]King, *Trumpet of Conscience*, 71.

affects all indirectly. We are made to live together because of the interrelated structure of reality."[13] In that same sermon, he cites the Bible and reminds his audience that "in Christ there is neither male nor female,"[14] a point that would have been good for him to have extended to the treatment of women in the civil rights movement. So many of King's statements are entrenched in gender-binary language that, though jarring for us to read today, were typical of his time. How powerful would it have been for him to say, "man and woman"? To say, "In Christ all people are equal"? Or to acknowledge through public action, like elevating the women in the Black freedom movement, that there is neither male nor female in Christ?

King's perspective that all life is interrelated and connected is not unique to *The Trumpet of Conscience.* He makes a similar point in "Letter from a Birmingham Jail": "Whatever affects one directly, affects all directly." In other words, our proximity as a beloved community demands that we root out all forms of injustice regardless of how they manifest. In this letter, King also deems social analysis that "deals merely with the effects and does not grapple with the underlying causes" as superficial. Examining the system and grappling with why it is the way it is involves studying history and power. As Austin Channing Brown expresses poignantly, "Our only chance at dismantling racial injustice is being more curious about its origins than we are about our comfort."[15] She understands that God does not care about our comfort. God is shaping our character, and to do so requires us to become uncomfortable. Doing the work of justice also requires that we be uncomfortable. Indeed, if everything is interrelated, as King noted, we have to include topics like gender injustice, homophobic and transphobic violence, gender-based violence, and sexual harassment in our pursuit of justice.

Martin Luther King does not make the point only once that everything interrelates; he insists on it throughout *The Trumpet*

---

[13]King, *Trumpet of Conscience,* 71.

[14]King, *Trumpet of Conscience,* 74.

[15]Austin Channing Brown, *I'm Still Here: Black Dignity in a World Made for Whiteness* (New York: Convergent Books, 2018), 116.

of Conscience. Many points that King makes suggest that he may have understood and perhaps even agreed with the central tenets of intersectionality, such as the interlocking systems of oppression. When he calls unemployment one of the worst consequences of discrimination, he is acknowledging a system in which race and class are intertwined.[16] He even names such acknowledgment as a prerequisite for peace: "We aren't going to have peace on earth until we recognize this basic fact of the interrelated structure of all reality."[17] When I hear the phrase, "the interrelated structure of all reality," I am reminded of intersectionality and the work it allows us to do in the movement for justice everywhere. When King refers to peace, it can be defined as the absence of war. If we were to expand our definition of peace to include local communities and individuals, how might the goal of creating peace transform our lives? Sadly, I am not sure that peace is still the goal today. Sexual violence marginalizes survivors. Pushed to the margins, they are disbelieved and made to wonder if what they experienced actually happened.

THE TENSION BETWEEN JUSTICE AND INJUSTICE

References to the "beloved community" were instrumental in underlining that the purpose of the movement was not only victory but justice and reconciliation. King often framed this idea as an investment in "the beloved community." As he noted in an essay on nonviolence and racial injustice, "Our goal is to create a beloved community and this will require a qualitative change in our souls as well as a quantitative change in our lives."[18] King explains this further when he states that in Montgomery, specifically, "tension in

---

[16]See King, *Trumpet of Conscience*, 11, where he states that "intimately related to discrimination is one of its worst consequences—unemployment."

[17]King, *Trumpet of Conscience*, 72.

[18]Martin Luther King Jr., "Nonviolence: The Only Road to Freedom," May 4, 1966, https://teachingamericanhistory.org.

this city is not between white people and [Black] people. The tension is, at bottom, between justice and injustice, between the forces of light and the forces of darkness. And, if there is a victory, it will be a victory not merely for fifty thousand Negroes, but a victory for justice and the forces of light. We are out to defeat injustice and not white persons who may be unjust."[19]

The notion of the beloved community resonates with Alicia Garza's love letter to Black people, in which she writes "Black lives matter" for the first time. It was her investment in her own beloved community that motivated her to write the letter that launched the movement. But the presence of all forms of gender-based violence also prevents us from achieving the goal of beloved community.

Certainly, embracing forgiveness and reconciliation is difficult, especially when we consider perpetrators of sexual violence. What does it mean to fight against rape as an injustice rather than against the individual perpetrators of that injustice? This is an area of my Christian faith with which I really wrestle. How do I invite the person who raped one of my friends to be in beloved community? How can I, like Bryan Stevenson, reach the point of not just believing but behaving as though "a person is more than the worst thing that they have ever done"? I don't want to be in beloved community with rapists, child sexual abusers, and pedophile priests. I prefer to admonish them in a similar way to Jesus: "If any of you put a stumbling block before one of these little ones who believe in me, it would be better for you if a great millstone were fastened around your neck and you were drowned in the depth of the sea" (Matt 18:6). King's mandate to turn the other cheek does not equip me here. I can't wrap my mind around what else to do with perpetrators of sexual violence unless I consider the idea of restorative justice. In connecting sexual violence and restorative justice, I am guided by the filmmaker and activist Aishah Shahidah Simmons. Simmons's Love WITH Accountability movement invites survivors of sexual abuse to envision a world that

---

[19]Martin Luther King Jr., "The Christian Way of Life in Human Relations, Address Delivered at the General Assembly of the National Council of Churches," St. Louis, Missouri, December 4, 1957, https://kinginstitute.stanford.edu.

ends sexual abuse without relying on the criminal justice system. She offers a model based on restorative justice that repairs the harm caused by a crime by inviting community members to participate in the process and to present their vision for justice.

Restorative Justice

Activists are championing models of restorative justice to replace the criminal justice system—which, as activists have noted, is a misnomer in and of itself since it does so much to advance injustice rather than justice—as one pathway of justice for survivors of sexual violence. Restorative justice requires that perpetrators admit, acknowledge, and express remorse for the harm that they inflict on survivors. The process of reconciliation can only begin with the admission and acknowledgment of harm by the perpetrator. The goal of the movement is truly to restore and repair rather than to discipline and punish. This is a more inclusive and viable model for survivors in Black and Brown communities especially because the silences that shroud sexual violence in this context are often informed by the extant criminalization of Black and Brown men that drives survivors into silence rather than seek any form of redress. With a reimagined criminal justice system and the abolition of prisons—which we discuss at length in the next chapter—survivors can find alternative paths to justice. That work is only possible with the initiative and the advocacy of survivors themselves.

Faith, Gender, and Justice

Nevertheless, we cannot discuss how *The Trumpet of Conscience* can be applied to the movement to end gender-based violence without considering how King figures in the movement for gender equality. Although Martin Luther King states that "every man is somebody because he is a child of God,"[20] in reality, little in his life

---

[20]King, *Trumpet of Conscience*, 74.

or in his writings demonstrated how his thoughts about our common humanity extended to women. My gender-neutral interpretation of this idea is that "every human is somebody because they are a child of God." Reverend King's abiding Christian faith led him to cite Jesus Christ often as an example of the way, although he never explored or discussed these ways in terms of thwarting the cultural disregard for women. The original statement that every "man is somebody" is well aligned with a masculine and patriarchal view that characterized King and those who surrounded him, especially in the context of both the civil rights movement and the Black church.

Erica Edwards explores and exposes how heteropatriarchy was reproduced by King as well as in how he is remembered.[21] Writing about charisma as a political fiction or ideal, Edwards helps to inform my own view, which is wary of how King is remembered and concerned about what and who are left out when catapulting one leader to the highest position of exclusive importance. "The charismatic structure of Black churches came to dominate the Black political imagination," to the point that there was no room to imagine civil rights leaders as anything other than Black and male, contrary to the participation of Black women.[22] The sexism within the civil rights movement has been well documented. Journalist Paul Delaney correctly notes, "The civil rights movement was run as a male preserve. . . . Women were there . . . but within defined roles that allowed men to lead."[23] Moreover, knowing what we know about King today, he clearly would have rejected his own deification. Still, King's treatment of women, or his unabashed noninclusiveness, is disappointing when we consider his deep faith and actions motivated by a relationship with Jesus. In fact, who better to help us appreciate the importance of women and girls than Jesus Christ himself?

Throughout the Gospels, we see Jesus noticing women, talking

---

[21]Erica Edwards, *Charisma and the Fictions of Black Leadership* (Minneapolis: University of Minnesota Press, 2018), 5.

[22]Edwards, *Charisma*, 5.

[23]Paul Delaney, "Dorothy Height and the Sexism of the Civil Rights Movement," The Root, May 12, 2010, https://www.theroot.com.

to women, taking instructions from women, inviting women to the table, exhorting women, sitting with women, lifting women up, affirming women, restoring women, claiming women, pointing to women as positive examples, and forgiving women. Jesus treats women with respect and honor. Jesus is inclusive. His ministry included women. The first time he reveals himself as the Messiah in Luke, it is to a woman. The first to learn of his resurrection are women. The first miracle he performs is because a woman (his mother) tells him to do so. At one point, in both Mark and Matthew, a woman gets Jesus to change his mind about whether or not to heal her daughter. Jesus treated women in ways that were completely countercultural for his deeply patriarchal society, where the status of women was inferior. Jesus's treatment of women was nothing short of revolutionary. With Jesus as our example, it becomes clear that gender-based violence is a social justice issue that our faith demands us to see. Given King's robust faith and his incisive attention to the social, political, and economic evils that plagued American society, his inattention to women's rights is curious and lacking.

As a former member of the Student Nonviolent Coordinating Committee (SNCC), Gwendolyn Zoharah Simmons has discussed at length the sexism within the civil rights movement and the silence regarding the treatment of women. She writes, "One of the things that we often don't talk about, but there was sexual harassment that often happened toward the women. And so, that was one of the things that, you know, I took a stand on, that, 'This was not—we're not going to get a consensus on this. There is not going to be sexual harassment of any of the women on this project or any of the women in this community. And you will be put out if you do it.'"[24] By calling out the issue of harassment of women and taking a stance against it, Simmons was able to create change that was truly countercultural.

Perhaps the question I am also wrestling with here is why gender-based violence is not seen as a justice or human rights issue central

---

[24]"Women in the Civil Rights Movement," Library of Congress, https://www.loc.gov.

to our faith. Is it because we live in a patriarchal society in which the needs of women are rarely met with political mobilization? Is it because women are still grossly undervalued? Black women's lives matter. Still, so often in the movement for Black lives it seems that Black women are erased and unaccounted for. Our labor matters, our organizing matters, and our innovation matters. Yet the fact that our lives do not seem to matter is revealed again and again when we see no mobilization around our deaths. The case of Breonna Taylor in 2020 is making small inroads into this situation. Her name is being said. Breonna's Law, for example, was passed in her name. Still, the mobilization around her death is simply not the same—and the male police officers who were responsible for killing her in her apartment had not yet been charged even more than one hundred days after her murder. When one was finally arrested, no charges ended up being filed despite the convening of the grand jury. In many ways, Breonna Taylor has not received the recognition she deserves. This is why we must emphasize the insight of the Combahee River Collective to remind people that "to be recognized as human, levelly human, is enough."[25]

While King had a rich faith that informed his understanding of justice and determination to realize a better society, he was also critical of the Black church. In fact, during his lifetime, King was one of its foremost critics. "Although he often criticized Black Christians for their complacency, King never disowned either the Black church movement or his own early faith commitments. He deepened their intellectual grounding, but he never belittled the faith of the people or their powerful spirituality."[26] King's critique of the Black church suggests further that he could have paid greater attention to sexism and misogyny, but willingness to address the treatment of women as a human rights issue did not extend that far.

---

[25]Combahee River Collective Statement, www.blackpast.org.
[26]James Melvin Washington, *A Testament of Hope: The Essential Writings and Speeches of Martin Luther King, Jr.* (New York: HarperCollins, 1991), xi.

THE ME TOO MOVEMENT

Like Black Lives Matter, the Me Too movement represents one of the most pressing global social justice struggles of the twenty-first century. Often described as a "reckoning with sexual violence" in ways similar to how Black Lives Matter is called "a reckoning with race," its focus—addressing sexual harassment and sexual violence—can broadly be understood as a movement to end gender-based violence against all people. As a gender justice initiative, the Me Too movement calls attention to how sexism operates perniciously in daily life. Although it was catapulted into fame in 2017, the movement began with Tarana Burke in the early 2000s. "Me Too" grew out of Burke's work with young Black girls in the South. As an activist and organizer Tarana Burke worked extensively around the country to help young people in marginalized communities. While she was working at a youth camp in Alabama, she became close to a thirteen-year-old girl. During one of their private conversations, the girl, whom Burke refers to as Heaven, disclosed that she was a survivor of sexual violence. Tarana Burke's response was not what one would expect from an internationally known advocate for survivors of and organizers against sexual violence. Rather than embrace Heaven, she rejected her and sent her to someone else. That moment of rejection continued to haunt Tarana Burke because the girl never returned to the youth camp, and to this day, Burke does not know what happened to Heaven. Feeling incredibly guilty about her reaction, Burke asked herself, "Why couldn't I just have said me too?" The idea of "me too" then became an animating force and the rallying call for the movement that Burke subsequently founded.

Using the framework of "empowerment through empathy," Burke tapped into why it is difficult for people to see themselves in and as survivors. She challenged people to learn to say, "Me too," and to use empathy as a point of departure for changing the culture in discussing rape. Describing how she founded the movement, Burke explains: " 'Me too' is so powerful because somebody had said it to me and it changed the trajectory of my healing process once I heard that. 'Me too' was about reaching the places that other people wouldn't go, bringing messages and words and encouragement to survivors of sexual violence where other people wouldn't be talking about it."[27] Founded to help organizations fighting sexual violence—especially against Black women and girls, and other women of color from low-income communities—the goal of #MeToo is to promote healing. Tarana Burke first coined the term "Me Too" and created an organization around it in order to support young Black girl survivors of sexual violence. Burke used the model of healing through empathy as the foundation of her organization.

Empathy

Tarana Burke's retelling of how Me Too began exemplifies the analogy we noted earlier with the parable of the Good Samaritan that King refers to in "I've Been to the Mountaintop." Here, King explains that whereas the people who walk by the man on the road ask themselves, "What will happen to me if I stop for him?," the Good Samaritan asks, "What will happen to *him* if I do not stop to help him?" The essential difference between the two responses lies in empathy. As Michelle Alexander explains in *The New Jim Crow*, the failure to care leads us to turn our eyes away from injustice in every form. Empathy equips us to look through new eyes. We suffer with those who are suffering as though we ourselves are suffering. Empathy means that we care and that we have deep compassion. Empathy means that we are not motivated by whether something has happened or can happen to us personally. Our concern should be for every individual, including and perhaps especially those who are most vulnerable and most marginalized.

The story behind the second phase of the Me Too movement, with which most people are familiar, begins in October 2016, when

---

[27]Sameer Rao, interview with Tarana Burke, *Color Lines*, October 17, 2017, www.colorlines.com.

Alyssa Milano posted a challenge on social media: raise your hand if you have ever been sexually assaulted or harassed and respond with #MeToo. Alyssa Milano's tweet resonated with women throughout the world, causing, in just hours, the hashtag to go viral. Taken together, the words "Me too" became a household term popularized especially in 2016 after the allegations against Hollywood producer Harvey Weinstein were made public, as dozens of women accused him of sexual assault, rape, and harassment.

Although Martin Luther King rarely spoke about women, women's rights, sexism, or what Moya Bailey has termed *misogynoir* (misogyny against Black women), applying *The Trumpet of Conscience* in the twenty-first century requires taking seriously the problem of gender-based violence. It is a human rights abuse that should be considered a major social justice cause. In his "Christmas Sermon on Peace," King writes, "What if brotherhood was more than a few words at the end of a prayer, but rather the first order of business of every legislative agenda?"[28]

Consequently, what if our care, compassion, and concern for fellow humans were the first orders of business of every legislative agenda? What if we went beyond #MeToo to really care for survivors and incorporate their needs into our culture? To do so would not only transform but dismantle rape culture. It would entail imagining a world without sexual violence—in which survivors are believed, and where women and girls and transgender people do not have to fear for their safety.

Changing Rape Culture

In teaching, I create spaces to allow students to take rape culture seriously as a justice issue. *Rape culture* is defined as a society or environment in which rape is prevalent and sexual violence is normalized by the media and popular culture and through social norms. For the past few years, I have been teaching a class that takes on the

---

[28]King, *Trumpet of Conscience*, 79.

topic of rape culture with this transformation in mind. As I mentioned in the previous chapter, the class "Where #BlackLivesMatter Meets #MeToo" is co-taught with a sociologist colleague as part of our university's "Complex Problems Core," in which professors address a complex social problem and encourage students to consider possible solutions. We take on the problem of rape culture in multiple contexts—the United States, the Caribbean, and the African continent—and deploy interdisciplinary methodologies from the humanities and the social sciences. Our goal was to approach rape culture as an urgent global problem and equip students to imagine solutions for intervening in and eventually eradicating rape culture. The idea for the class was inspired by the book *Transforming a Rape Culture*.[29] In that book's preamble, the editors explain, "Transforming a rape culture involves imaginative leaps from our present state of institutionalized violence to a future that is safer and more just. We must summon our imaginations for this task, because history and society have so few precedents for us. . . . Transforming a rape culture is about changing fundamental attitudes and values." We took this statement seriously, and our students not only learned about the wide-ranging manifestations and ramifications of rape culture but were also asked to *summon their imaginations* to envision a world without sexual violence and to consider how to challenge the norms that perpetuate rape culture.

In this interdisciplinary class, we assign critical readings from the fields of sociology, literary, and cultural studies. We read articles and fiction by authors from the United States, Haiti, South Africa, Zimbabwe, and Rwanda. We watch films such as *NO! The Rape Documentary*, about sexual violence in the Black community; *The Hunting Ground*, about the widespread problem of campus sexual assault; and *Spotlight*, about how the *Boston Globe* unearthed the sex-abuse scandal in the Catholic Church. We ask questions including the following:

---

[29]Emilie Buchwald, Pamela Fletcher, and Martha Roth, eds., *Transforming a Rape Culture* (New York: Milkweed Editions, 1995).

- How do historical racialized, sexualized, and gendered tropes help us understand current-day responses to sexual assault?
- How do definitions of what constitutes sexual violence shape how we respond to survivors and perpetrators?
- Why is rape culture so pervasive around the world?
- How do writers represent sexual violence in their fiction?
- What is the relationship between rape and representation?
- How do representations of rape differ across various media?
- How are rape victims and survivors portrayed in literature and film?
- How do cultural workers reflect, challenge, or attempt to dismantle some of the basic premises of rape culture through their representations of sexual violence?

Given the statistical reality that one in five college women will be raped in the span of their four years in college, we understand that the work we do in class extends beyond our students' imaginations. Many of them have had experiences of sexual violence or have loved ones who are survivors themselves. Therefore, our students draw from their experiential knowledge, but some of them will also be triggered and traumatized by the materials we explore in class. In light of this reality we also expose students to the many resources available to survivors and explain the importance of self-care for people working in the field. Teaching the class requires my co-teacher and me to put ourselves in the position of the Samaritan and ask, "If we do not help these students, what will happen to them?" Furthermore, we want the class to serve as a springboard for young people to become antirape advocates who will transform the world and actively imagine a world without sexual violence. We want to arouse empathy in our students so that when they encounter young people like Heaven they will not shrink away, but run toward and lean into her pain appropriately. They will activate their own empathy and draw from the wells of their experiences and knowledge.

The class also includes a weekly lab that involves collaborative work concerning historical and contemporary cases of sexual violence or working with local antiviolence organizations in the Boston area. In these labs, students connect the class texts and contemporary manifestations of rape culture, such as the crisis of campus sexual assault, sexual abuse in the Catholic Church, and the proliferation of sexual violence in refugee camps. By linking the study of rape culture to modern-day occurrences, the students are better equipped to create projects that intervene in the problem of sexual violence. The final element of the class structure is a weekly reflection in which we consider specific cases of sexual violence—through films, speakers, and panel discussions. During these two-hour evening sessions, we invite local community organizations, such as Black Lives Matter Boston and the Boston Area Rape Crisis Center, as well as nationally known leaders in the movement to end violence against women and girls, such as Scheherazade and Salamishah Tillet, the cofounders of A Long Walk Home, and the activist and filmmaker Aishah Shahidah Simmons, who directed *NO! The Rape Documentary* and authored *Love WITH Accountability*, a practical guide for dealing with sexual violence within families and communities.

Our goal is for the students to imagine a world without sexual violence and actively devise ways to intervene in, address, and ultimately end rape culture, and to equip students to consider the problem of sexual violence from a perspective that is informed and empathetic, as well as activist-minded. Descriptions of this class and its objectives are important because the class represents an effort for young people to engage rape culture as an issue of social justice. Ultimately, the class invites the students to ask themselves, "If I do not stand with the rape survivors, what will happen to them?," reminding them that rape culture is a justice issue that requires collective attention and organizing.

Tarana Burke's pointed focus on justice embraces an ethic with "the least of these" at the center. She is attempting to create more justice in a world that too often ignores Black women and girls. Working with Black and Brown girls to speak healing into their lives, remind them that healing is possible, and place survivors at the center of the movement has been one of Burke's goals through the Me Too movement. Tarana Burke has repeatedly stated that the movement is "not about men being brought down. The goal is for justice to happen, for culture to change and to support survivors."[30] She also underlines that #MeToo is not a movement for women but a movement for all survivors—it includes men, boys, and transgender people who are also victims of sexual violence. The movement makes clear that we must not only believe survivors but amplify their voices and follow their lead.

#MeToo is also a twenty-first-century movement that is illustrative of the moment in which we live. Through the use of the phrase "Empowerment through empathy," we are reminded that our feelings and how we respond to what bothers us can be deployed in service of social justice projects. It is also an example of survivor advocacy. With survivor advocates at the center of the movement for ending violence against women and girls, we see how the revolution of values that King describes in *The Trumpet of Conscience* can occur. Finally, #MeToo demonstrates the importance of narrative and witness: the use of stories to create change.

SOUNDING THE TRUMPET

While Tarana Burke is the founder of #MeToo, she is not the first example of a Black woman organizing against sexual violence. Black women have been saying, "Me too," for centuries. The long history of Black women fighting sexual violence and framing it as a social justice issue confirms that Black women's advocacy and intervention have long paid attention to the intersections of racial justice and gender justice.

During slavery, when enslaved women were raped by slave owners and forced to give birth to their children, they shared these stories of violence with one another. Here, the story of Harriet Ja-

---

[30]Kirsten Chuba, "Tarana Burke Says #MeToo Isn't About 'Taking Down Powerful Men'," https://variety.com/video/tarana-burke-metoo-powerful-men/.

cobs (1813–1897) is exemplary. Jacobs, an enslaved girl who was sexually assaulted repeatedly by her enslavers, went on to become an abolitionist and an author. Her account of her experience is one of the most comprehensive written by a woman. In *Incidents in the Life of a Slave Girl*, Jacobs relates her experience under the pseudonym of Linda Brent. Published in 1861, the same year that the Civil War began, it is the first example of a slave narrative written by a woman who offers a searing portrait of how chattel slavery was an institution of extreme and unrelenting violence.[31]

Jacobs offers an early example of Black women describing their experience of sexual violence to advocate for freedom; others who followed her also positioned themselves as antirape advocates. Similarly, Ida B. Wells-Barnett (1862–1931), the journalist and antilynching advocate, offers an early-twentieth-century model for breaking silences around sexual violence. Born an enslaved person a year before emancipation, Wells went on to become a researcher, journalist, and activist. She was one of the earliest examples of how to use the press and tell stories for Black people by Black people and often did so by acknowledging how racism, sexism, and violence overlapped. Whenever possible, Wells named the victims of racist violence and told their stories. In her journals, she deplored that her subjects would have otherwise been forgotten by all "save the night wind, no memorial service to bemoan their sad and horrible fate."[32] Through her writing and advocacy, Wells laboriously pursued the dismantling of rape culture, asking society to confront myths about rape. "Nobody in this section of the country believes the threadbare old lie that Negro men rape white women," Wells wrote.[33] In the twentieth century, another Black woman who said, "Me too," was civil rights activist Rosa Parks, whose work began with investigating

---

[31]Harriet A. Jacobs (Linda Brent), *Incidents in the Life of a Slave Girl* (Boston: Self-published, 1861).

[32]Ida B. Wells, "Southern Horrors: Lynch Law in All Its Phases" (1802), Digital History ID 3614, https://www.digitalhistory.uh.edu/disp_textbook_print.cfm?smtid=3&psid=3614.

[33]Wells, "Southern Horrors."

sexual violence in the 1950s, when she discovered the case of Recy Taylor, a black woman who was gang-raped by group of white men. Parks's beginnings as an antirape activist are well documented but rarely invoked. Danielle McGuire tells the story of Recy Taylor in *At the Dark End of the Street*, which exposes how Black women's experiences with sexual violence at the hands of white male perpetrators forever changed the trajectory of the civil rights movement.

Following Rosa Parks, there are numerous examples of Black women's activism and organizing against sexual violence. Professor Angela Davis was among the first to excavate the "myth of the Black male rapist" in her scholarship. Similarly, Anita Hill charted new ground in 1991 by daring to speak up about workplace harassment when she testified against Clarence Thomas. As these examples confirm, Black women for many decades have been saying, "Me too," and denouncing violence against Black women through their activism and advocacy.

One of the greatest successes of the Me Too movement has been to puncture the overwhelming silence in response to sexual violence. For the first time, a public national conversation about sexual violence is taking place. In the media, in the film industry, in churches, and in schools, people are calling out perpetrators and implementing ways to uplift the voices of survivors. In faith-based communities, the #MeToo chorus resulted in a small wave of activism. By way of conclusion, I want to end with an example of how Black women's activism against sexual violence is reaching previously eclipsed corners.

A few years ago, here in Boston I was invited to participate in the Shatter the Silence Ministry through Bethel AME Church. The church convenes a small group of people for whom ending gender-based violence represents a higher calling. For months we met as a small group and discussed how rape culture figures in the Bible, the church, and society at large. We studied Bible passages, talked about our experiences with these issues, and participated in healing circles as well as arts-based workshops in the community. We drew from resources such as Monica A. Coleman's *The Dinah Project:*

A Handbook for Congregational Response to Sexual Violence and looked to see what other churches throughout the country were explicitly addressing and intervening in rape culture. The following year we also embarked on antirape crisis counseling and advocacy training through the Boston Area Rape Crisis Center. One of our first public projects together was to create a "Me Too" service during which we put the problem of sexual violence at the center of Sunday's liturgy. We performed an original piece of performance art based on discussions and healing circles on which we had previously embarked. One of Bethel AME's copastors, Rev. Dr. Gloria White-Hammond, preached a powerful sermon about how rape culture is perpetuated from Judges 19. From the outset, we were purposeful and intentional about making this small group within the Shatter the Silence Ministry a place for healing, training, and teaching about sexual violence and trauma that not only supports survivors but also equips and empowers advocates to address sexual victimization. There is indeed a long way to go, but these examples show that we have a new generation of believers prepared to grapple with the subject of gender-based violence from many varied perspectives informed by a faith that does justice.

4

Ending Mass Incarceration

*If we want to imagine the possibility of a society with-
out racism, it has to be a society without prisons.*
                                            —Angela Davis

The first time I had to explain the inextricable link between justice and faith, it was during a presentation about social justice for
our church's youth group. I had prepared a lesson based on Jesus's
parable about the kingdom of God in which he uses the analogy of
separating the sheep from the goats. "'For I was hungry and you
gave me food, I was thirsty and you gave me something to drink,
I was a stranger and you welcomed me, I was naked and you gave
me clothing, I was sick and you took care of me, I was in prison and
you visited me'" (Matt 25:35–36). I asked the twelve teenagers in
the group to list all the needs that Jesus enumerates and then explain
how they could fulfill those needs today. Most of their answers were
straightforward. For the hungry: donate to a food bank or give a
sandwich to someone who is begging for money in front of a res-
taurant. To invite a stranger in: support an organization that works
with refugees, or better yet, invite a stranger over to your home! To
clothe the naked: give clothes to a local shelter. But there was one
that stumped some of them: "When I was in prison you came to visit
me." How do we visit those in prison? Or rather, why? "Why would

we do that? Aren't people in prisons bad?" The Black teenage boy asking the question had grown up in a family actively involved in many forms of service in the church. As a Black male, he belongs to the demographic that is overrepresented in the prison population, which made me feel like the stakes were particularly high as I mulled over possible responses to his provocative question. Without even attempting an explanation of prison abolition, I tried—awkwardly and unsuccessfully—to illuminate why Jesus encourages believers to visit those who are imprisoned. Fortunately, another student came to my rescue and began sharing about his mother's visits to a local prison. A young adult leader of the youth group then shared a story about how his own youth group used to play basketball with teenagers held in juvenile detention. "That's cool," my originally unconvinced interlocutor responded to the basketball game example. "We should do that." He was eventually compelled, and, dare I say of this skeptical teen, swayed by stories about developing a relationship with people who are imprisoned. Visiting those who are in prison makes no sense without real-life models of connection and proximity.

At the time, I did not consider engaging these young people on the topic of prison abolition, but in retrospect I wish that I had done so—because I now understand that prison abolition and Christian faith must go hand in hand.

PRISON ABOLITION

"Abolish prisons!" "End mass incarceration!" "Imagine a world without prisons." More than pithy slogans, these words designate a movement to end the prison system as we know it today. These are among the basic ideas espoused by prison abolitionists. In the mainstream, prison abolition has been represented as both radical and improbable. However, if we are to work toward justice and allow our imaginations to lead us as far as possible in realizing freedom for all people, prison abolition cannot remain on the periphery. If we take seriously the charge of continuing the struggle for Black freedom and seeing it through to completion, abolishing prisons should be a goal. But for most, imagining a world without prisons is far from intuitive. As activist, Black feminist scholar, and prison abolitionist Angela Davis specifies, "The prison is considered so natural and so normal that it is extremely hard to imagine life without them."[1] Prison abolitionists take what many see as too hard to imagine and work toward its realization. Sure of what they hope for and certain of what they do not see, modern-day prison abolitionists are propelled and inspired by conscience.

Creating a more just society means taking seriously the need to end mass incarceration, the roots of which are in white supremacy, poverty, and militarism. As Davis explains, "Abolition is about rethinking the kind of future we want: [the kind of] social future, economic future, political future, etc. . . . It is about revolution."[2] Following the logic that prison abolition *is* about revolution, it radically manifests the "true revolution of values" that King delineates in *The Trumpet of Conscience.* A more just world is, without question, a world without prisons. Mass incarceration is an urgent racial and economic justice problem because the prison population is overwhelmingly poor, Black, and Brown. It is a justice issue because prisons deny people of their dignity and humanity. The incarceration of a disproportionate number of Black and Brown people in the United States rightfully incites people committed to antiracism, and indeed, the numbers of the incarcerated represent a deep moral failure on our society's part.

The *prison-industrial complex* (PIC) is a term created by antiprison activists to refer to the widespread harm of mass incarceration.[3] They define *PIC abolition* as "a political vision with the goal of eliminating imprisonment, policing, and surveillance and creating

---

[1]Angela Davis, *Are Prisons Obsolete?* (New York: Seven Stories, 2003), 10.

[2]"Angela Davis on Abolition, Calls to Defund Police, Toppled Racist Statues & Voting in 2020 Election," YouTube.com, July 3, 2020, https://www.youtube.com/watch?v=N7RPQo0LW-I&feature=emb_title.

[3]Critical Resistance, "What Is the PIC? What Is Abolition?" http://criticalresistance.org.

alternatives to punishment and imprisonment."[4] This definition is useful in that it highlights the inextricable link between the prison-industrial complex and militarism and capitalism—two systems that King attacked vociferously and consistently. If we were to take seriously the charge to create a more just society, then we have to attend to the problem of mass incarceration. Prison abolition does more than simply posit a solution to mass incarceration; it is a "theory of change" that asks us to imagine a world without prisons and how to create it. As such, it necessarily involves dismantling *and* building. Prison abolition offers clear alternatives rooted in changing the world by investing in communities and local programs rather than funneling more money into prisons and funding police at alarmingly high levels. A world without prisons privileges the needs of the beloved community and places marginalized people at the center. When viewed through a lens of prison abolitionism, this beloved community is what abolitionist educator Bettina Love describes as "a community that strives for economic, housing, racial, health, and queer justice and citizenship for all."[5]

Thinking alongside King's quest for freedom and clarion call to conscience suggests that prison abolition would have been on his agenda. Without even considering how many times he himself was targeted by an unjust and unequal criminal justice system, we know that, at the most basic level, Dr. Martin Luther King Jr. was for the liberation of all oppressed people. As such, his devotion to "the least of these" means that mass incarceration is an issue that he would champion today. When we approach prison abolition from the perspective of Christian faith, its inconsistency with what we believe is particularly egregious. Prisons perpetuate the false notion that people are disposable. For followers of Jesus, prisons are a problem with which our faith must reckon. Jesus often referred to setting the captives free: " 'The Spirit of the Lord is upon me, because he has anointed me to bring good news to the poor. He has

---

[4]"Critical Resistance, "What Is the PIC?"

[5]Bettina A. Love, *We Want to Do More Than Survive: Abolitionist Teaching and the Pursuit of Educational Freedom* (Boston: Beacon Press, 2020), 7.

sent me to proclaim release to the captives and recovery of sight to the blind, to let the oppressed go free'" (Luke 4:18). It is not a stretch to say that followers of Jesus should be prison abolitionists, yet prison abolition or any form of attention to mass incarceration and how it has ravaged Black and poor communities, in particular, is rarely on church agendas.[6]

While some churches have prison ministry programs, few have wholeheartedly taken up the cause of prison abolition. Nevertheless, there have been powerful articulations of faith-mandated prison abolition that emerged as early as the 1970s. In 1976, Quaker prison minister Fay Honey Knopp (1918–1995) and a group of activists published a modest booklet titled *Instead of Prisons: A Handbook for Abolitionists*. This slim volume outlined three main goals: to establish a moratorium on all new prison building; to "de-carcerate" those currently in prison; and to "ex-carcerate," which means to move away from criminalization and from the use of incarceration altogether. As the authors explain, "The abolitionist ideology is based on economic and social justice for all, concern for all victims, and reconciliation within a caring community."[7] The caring community to which they refer echoes King's use of *beloved community*, reminding us again how faith is fertile ground for planting, nourishing, and growing visions of prison abolition. A rare twenty-first-century and faith-based example continuing this vision is Christians for Abolition, an organization that uses biblical principles to support prison abolition. For example, they persuasively argue that "God desires a system of justice that occurs within relationship and results in healed and renewed relationships with the beloved community," and by demonstrating how the prison-industrial complex is in direct contradiction to it.[8] They quote the book of Exodus as an a priori example of the theological precedent for "releasing the captives," explaining that the Jewish people in

---

[6]See Christians for the Abolition of Prisons, https://christiansforabolition.org.

[7]"Preface," Instead of Prisons, www.prisonpolicy.org.

[8]See Christians for the Abolition of Prisons, https://christiansforabolition.org. I am grateful to Tara Edelschick for bringing this organization to my attention.

Egypt were both enslaved and imprisoned. Scripture is rife with examples in support of prison abolition. To suffer with those who are suffering, as though we ourselves are suffering, is to recognize that mass incarceration grossly perpetuates racial and economic injustice in our society. The Letter to the Hebrews is also unambiguous in this regard: "Remember those who are in prison, as though you were in prison with them; those who are being tortured, as though you yourselves were being tortured" (13:3). In other words, to listen to and be guided by a trumpet of conscience in the twenty-first century is to espouse the goal of prison abolition.

The ability of prisons to "facilitate the disappearing of people" should shock us into action. But our sick society seems indifferent to that disappearing.[9] Furthermore, the history of prisons in the United States reveals that the system of mass incarceration thriving today began with a racist premise. Like the current police system, prisons were created in the aftermath of slavery to discipline and to punish. Legal scholar and author Michelle Alexander argues passionately that "no task is more urgent for racial justice advocates today than ensuring that America's current racial caste system is its last."[10] She pursues that "urgent cause" by exploring the modern antiprison movement as another twenty-first-century example of the trumpet of conscience that loudly beckons us. By placing scholars and activists like Angela Davis, Ruth Wilson Gilmore, and Mariame Kaba in conversation with King's call to peace, I show that paying attention to the trumpet of conscience today must include the end of mass incarceration and prisons in order to build a better world.

Like the Black Lives Matter and Me Too movements, the modern prison abolition movement is powered by the unrelenting activism of women of color. Dedicated to intersectional social justice, these women adhere to Black feminist politics that are radically inclusive; living out Fannie Lou Hamer's premise that "nobody's free until everybody's free," their goal has always been freedom for all. While

---

[9]Davis, *Are Prisons Obsolete?*

[10]Michelle Alexander, *The New Jim Crow: Mass Incarceration in the Age of Colorblindness* (New York: New Press, 2012), 19.

many rightfully locate the origins of antiprison activism earlier in the twentieth century, today Ruth Wilson Gilmore, Angela Davis, and Mariame Kaba are championing this work in unprecedented ways. Of course, the language of abolition purposefully parallels the centuries-old movement against slavery and racist oppression. Although prison abolition is a struggle with a long history, in many ways these women were among the first to introduce and imagine prison abolition in explicit relation to the freedom struggle. By connecting prison abolition to a global freedom movement, they are demonstrating that "freedom is a constant struggle" and that, despite the gains of the civil rights movement, much work remains to be done.[11]

Sounding the Trumpet

Along with Rachel Herzing, Gilmore and Davis are the cofounders of Critical Resistance, an international movement to dismantle the prison-industrial complex. In their work, they refer to the *prison-industrial complex* as "the overlapping interests of government and industry that use surveillance, policing, and imprisonment as solutions to economic, social, and political problems."[12] The term intentionally emphasizes the corporatization of prisons, which has made the system far more financially supported, entrenched, and militarized today. Referring to prisons as an industry highlights the billions of dollars associated with their continued creation and maintenance.[13] Critical Resistance participates in a global struggle against injustice whose goal is to eliminate all forms of oppression and promote freedom. What I like about the organization's name is how it evokes the need to be critically minded about the proliferation of prisons in our society. Critique paired with resistance is another

---

[11]Davis, *Freedom Is a Constant Struggle.*

[12]See Critical Resistance, http://criticalresistance.org.

[13]According to Bettina Love, in *We Want to Do More Than Survive*, "Prisons bring in $70 billion a year in revenue, and its industry spends $45 million a year lobbying to keep people incarcerated and for longer sentences" (11).

hallmark of the movement to end mass incarceration and why the work of prison abolitionists begins by encouraging us to think differently about prisons; Critical Resistance invites us to ask different questions. Angela Davis calls us to question our assumptions about why prisons exist and how they function in our society. The title of her book—*Are Prisons Obsolete?*—is far from a rhetorical question; in it she makes the case for eliminating prisons.

To explain the goals of the prison abolition movement for a group of middle-school children, anti-prison activist and academic Ruth Wilson Gilmore suggests that "instead of asking whether anyone should be locked up or go free, why don't we think about why we solve problems by repeating the kind of behavior that brought us the problem in the first place?"[14] In other words, by asking why a system exists, we can better understand why it should end. Put differently, a focus on prisons as an apparatus rather than on people who are imprisoned interrogates the entire system rather than individual behavior. This premise recalls some of King's cogent arguments about systemic injustice in *The Trumpet of Conscience*. Although he does not explicitly name white supremacy, he explains that "it is not the race per se that we fight but the policies and ideology that leaders of that race have formulated to perpetuate oppression," effectively indicting a system of racist oppression at work,[15] or as Ella Baker claims more vigorously, to understand the problem in its fullness, "we must go down to the root." Prison abolition thus begs the question: when we examine the root of prisons as a form of discipline and punishment, what effects are they actually having on our society?

As a practice, prison abolition encompasses nuances that have often been oversimplified. First, it asks that we understand prisons as a "false solution" to the problems we face as a society.[16] Second, prison abolition focuses not only on dismantling but on building. Third, it is preoccupied by the imagination, encouraging us

---

[14] Ruth Wilson Gilmore, "Is Prison Necessary? Ruth Wilson Gilmore Might Change Your Mind," *New York Times Magazine*, April 17, 2019.

[15] King, *Trumpet of Conscience*, 9.

[16] Davis, *Freedom Is a Constant Struggle*, 6.

to think critically and imagine differently. As a global movement against all forms of oppression, prison abolition emblematizes the imperative for systemic change that is interconnected and international. Ending mass incarceration can lead to widespread systemic change in serving people on the margins. Envisioning some of these possibilities that stem from the end of prisons, Angela Davis lists "demilitarization of schools, revitalization of education at all levels, a health system that provides free physical and mental care to all, and a justice system based on reparation and reconciliation rather than retribution."[17] The trumpet is blowing. Will we hear its sound?

Who are these women, and how is their work extending a Black freedom struggle propelled by racial and economic justice? One of the trumpet players blowing loudly in the prison abolition orchestra is Ruth Wilson Gilmore.[18] Her interventions as an academic and an activist are paving the way for an abolitionist vision of freedom in the twenty-first century. In 1998 Davis and Gilmore, along with a group of people in the Bay Area, founded Critical Resistance. Gilmore's book *Golden Gulag: Prisons, Surplus, and Opposition in Globalizing California* (2007) is a rigorous study of how mass incarceration has shaped and reshaped the state of California. Gilmore argues convincingly that "racism is the state-sanctioned and/ or extralegal production and exploitation of group-differentiated vulnerability to premature death. Prison expansion is a new iteration of this theme."[19] Gilmore's exposure of the prisonization of the United States centers the voices of those most affected by it. In particular, she follows a group of poor Black women whose sons are victims of the prison-industrial complex.

Mariame Kaba is another dynamic activist at the forefront of the prison abolition movement who constantly urges that hope be central

---

[17]Davis, *Are Prisons Obsolete?*, 107.

[18]As the author of *Golden Gulag: Prisons, Surplus, and Opposition in Globalizing California* (Berkeley, CA: University of California Press, 2007) and cofounder of groups like the California Prison Moratorium Project, whose mission is to suspend the construction of new prisons over a five-year period, Gilmore is a scholar-activist par excellence.

[19]Gilmore, *Golden Gulag,* 247.

to ending mass incarceration. The child of immigrants, Kaba was raised in New York City. Then she moved to Chicago where she worked as an educator and organizer for twenty years. In addition to being a prominent prison abolitionist, she is the founder of Project NIA, a grassroots organization with a vision to end youth incarceration.[20] Kaba's philosophy of justice strikingly echoes Martin Luther King's vision. As she explains, prison abolition is a collective project with a holistic approach to justice. In other words, everything is connected. As Kaba articulates, "Abolition is a collective project, not an individual project, which means that one person is not responsible for coming up with the solution."[21] For Kaba and other abolitionists, the goal is not only to entirely dismantle prisons but to create the conditions so that those institutions do not have to exist. By this she means that if people have fair wages, health care, access to education, and healthy living environments, then everyone in the society can flourish and the prison system would not need to exist. In other words, the call for prison abolition is a call for a more just world that removes every obstacle so that all people have what they need and the ability to flourish. Compellingly, Kaba repeatedly refers to "hope as a discipline" and encourages people who care about social justice to imagine the kind of world they want to inhabit. She asks, "How do you define the world you want to create, the world you want to build, the world you want to live in?"[22] and encourages us all to imagine, to dream, and to envision in ways that bring to my mind King's most famous speech, in which he describes the world in which he wants to live. As Gilmore reiterates, "Abolitionists are everything-ist," meaning that they take a complete and holistic view of justice. Fannie Lou Hamer's statement that "nobody is free until everybody is free" remains the guiding principle that reminds us

---

[20]Project NIA is an American advocacy organization that supports youth in trouble with the law, as well as those victimized by violence and crime, through community-based alternatives as opposed to formal legal proceedings. This project is aiming to end juvenile incarceration. See www.project-nia.org.

[21]Mariame Kaba, *We Do This 'Til We Free Us: Abolitionist Organizing and Transforming Justice* (Chicago: Haymarket Books, 2021), 110.

[22]Kaba, *We Do This 'Til We Free Us*, 27.

that prison abolition is about so much more than prisons—it is about creating a just society for all, valuing all lives equally, and ensuring that everyone is free. Gilmore quotes the prison abolitionist and scholar James Forman, who wrote *Locking Up Our Own: Crime and Punishment in Black America*: "What I love about abolition is the idea that you imagine a world without prisons, and then you have to build that world."[23] Forman's point picks up where King left off in his "I Have a Dream" speech by asking us to imagine the world and then put the effort into realizing it. In other words, the dream is not enough on its own. Only the work—organizing, advocating, creating, building, and struggling—can realize the dream.

Among the awe-inspiring women doing the work of prison abolition in ways consistent with this struggle for freedom, Angela Yvonne Davis is a ubiquitous force. Her views align particularly well with the arguments presented in *The Trumpet of Conscience* in their commitment to a global, interconnected, and anticapitalist movement. While she gained notoriety in the 1970s for her activism when she was held as a political prisoner for over a year, in the twenty-first century she is a powerful and impassioned figure for a generation of millennial activists. As Barbara Ransby notes, "More than most other political celebrity figures of the twentieth century, Angela Davis has used her name and her fame in service of consciousness-raising, mobilizing, and organizing. And she has taken on controversial issues within Black progressive circles: feminist and queer politics, solidarity with Palestine, and prison abolition."[24] Through organizing, lecturing, and writing, Davis is a critical prison abolitionist voice. Her forceful arguments about mass incarceration as a moral failure establish the link between poverty, racism, and prisons. "Racism provides the fuel for maintenance, reproduction, and expansion of the prison-industrial complex."[25]

Like each of the movements explored in this book, the movement to end mass incarceration is explicitly global. Despite his vantage

---

[23]Gilmore, "Is Prison Necessary?"

[24]Ransby, *Making All Black Lives Matter*, 20.

[25]Davis, *Freedom Is a Constant Struggle*, 59.

point as an African American, in the world that King envisioned, the United States was not at the center. Many have identified his visit to India as the inspiration for his commitment to nonviolence, but importantly, King's global experiences were crucial to his development of a worldview that moved beyond the local. King was adamant that movements for social change must be international and was deeply critical of the United States' use of force throughout the world. His global vision was inspired by social movements worldwide, and for King, they were inextricably bound to the struggle against anti-Black racism in the United States. Motivated by a commitment to justice, rarely was he unable to connect the struggle for Black freedom to freedom struggles all over the world. For example, his global vision enabled him to critique imperialism with clarity: "We in the West must bear in mind that the poor countries are poor primarily because we have exploited them through political or economic colonialism. Americans in particular must help their nation repent of her modern economic imperialism. . . . So many of Latin America's problems have roots in the United States of America."[26]

The clarity with which he outlines the United States' nefarious implication and complicity in global injustice invites us to do the same today. Recognizing poverty as a global problem means examining the ways that the United States is complicit in maintaining power as the richest country in the world. Being the child of Haitian immigrants and a scholar of Africa and the Caribbean, I appreciate King's critique of the United States' global reach because I have seen its deleterious outcomes in many different contexts. From military occupation and support of malevolent dictators to neoliberal policies that thwart local economies, the United States has wreaked havoc on Haiti and countries like it throughout the Global South. For Latin American and Caribbean countries, the United States is known as the big bullying brother from the north who is always willing to use the powers of militarism and capitalism to secure power. The

---

[26]King, *Trumpet of Conscience*, 65

United States regularly deployed violence to advance its empire in Latin America and the Caribbean, including in nations like Haiti and Grenada where US invasions left lasting scars on those societies. As Lisa Harper explains, "Empire is the human compulsion to grow the bounds of the state's role and to exercise that role through domination, exploitation, and control."[27] King's internationally minded view of social justice allowed him to see the United States more clearly, illuminating his perspective on the United States as a "sick society." He understood that all oppressions can and should be linked, and he dug deeper into the root of problems to understand their origins. For example, regarding the war in Vietnam, King was not content to focus only on the conflict itself. In search of the deeper root, he concluded, "The war in Vietnam is but a symptom of a far deeper malady within the American spirit."[28]

That King vehemently argued positions against the Vietnam War demonstrates his ability to locate himself within a global struggle. This capacious view of justice refrains from only putting individuals at the center of the work. Instead, it privileges the collective that also allows for a more robust critique of systems. Again, the language of sickness that he often used reflects a problem far more profound than the government was willing to admit. When we place the problem of mass incarceration in a global context, we notice first that the "prison problem" in the United States can be considered as yet another manifestation of how the country traffics in force and fear to discipline its most marginalized citizens.

SEGREGATION AND INEQUALITY

The main objective of prison abolition is not reform; *to abolish* means to end entirely. The goal is to terminate unequivocally the use of prisons and the proliferation of the prison-industrial complex.

---

[27]Lisa Sharon Harper, *The Very Good Gospel: How Everything Wrong Can Be Made Right* (New York: Waterbrook, 2016), 161.

[28]King, *Trumpet of Conscience*, 32.

As Kaba explains, creating a world without prisons requires attending to and addressing all the inequities that structure our society so as to get to the root. Prison abolition imagines and seeks to bring about an entire world without prisons. Although Martin Luther King Jr. never specifically mentioned the end of prisons as a goal of the Black freedom movement, in its focus on the poor and marginalized *The Trumpet of Conscience* illustrates his preoccupations with the systems that undergird the logic of mass incarceration. In other words, King's commitment to exposing how poor, vulnerable, and marginalized communities were trapped in a system, out of which there appeared to be no way out, resonates with the problem of mass incarceration. He understood these challenges as systemic and endemic and called for deep-seated transformation of the system as the only true way to free the oppressed and marginalized from its snares. His metaphor of walls helps us to understand how he saw this system as constructed and pervasive: "The white power structure is still seeking to keep *the walls* of segregation and inequality substantially intact while [Black people's] determination to break through them has intensified."[29] The term *walls* reminds us that it is a system that was built and can only cease to exist if that system is torn down. As long as the walls remain intact, a portion of the population will remain trapped in the margins. The radical change that King was calling for required total demolition: the entire system must be destroyed.

Many scholars have explained that the system of mass incarceration that exists today was created in order to maintain the racial caste system in the United States. After enslavement, prisons were created as another tool of oppression to use against African Americans. Thinking about the prison as an institution also helps us to understand its longevity and sordid past in the United States. Mass incarceration is overwhelmingly biased against Black and Brown people, which is why anyone committed to ending racism must also be committed to ending prisons. But the prison-industrial complex

---

[29]King, *Trumpet of Conscience*, 9.

has become so encompassing, pervasive, and normalized in the United States that few question its existence or continuation. Considering this entrenched thinking, prison abolition calls us to think differently about mass incarceration. It is impossible to discuss the harm that prisons have done as an institution without also addressing the criminal justice system. Martin Luther King was painfully familiar with criminal justice in the United States. He was targeted by the FBI and arrested almost thirty times. In the United States, the idea of being a criminal has been systematically linked to Blackness.

Throughout *The Trumpet of Conscience*, King decries the hold of a system that even the accomplishments of desegregation could uproot. He never imagined desegregation as the antidote to racial injustice in the United States. This was the vision of the radical Dr. King, who, as we must not forget, was reviled by many while he lived. He was repeatedly arrested, incessantly tracked by the FBI, and eventually assassinated because of his radical views. Despite the sanitized view we have of King today, he was not interested in the individual acts of people, even those who came alongside him as antisegregationists. In this way, *The Trumpet of Conscience* affirms that individual acts were and still are insufficient for the realization of transformative change. "There must be *more than a statement* to the larger society; there must be a *force* that interrupts its functioning at some key point."[30] Justice requires deeply rooted transformation.

The demand for "more than a statement to the larger society" is reminiscent of how often today corporations, universities, school districts, and other institutions create systems and programs as a way to address the so-called racial pandemic. Throughout the country, new positions and programs are trumpeting a new commitment to antiracism—or rather, its distant and more benign cousins: diversity, equity, and inclusion. What is needed in all of these cases is more than a statement. A force that interrupts the functioning of these institutions will not come in the form of a program, task force, or committee; such a force needs to reach the root to dismantle the

---

[30]King, *Trumpet of Conscience*, 16.

entire system. Likewise, what is truly needed to end the injustice of mass incarceration is "a force that interrupts its functioning at some key point." Citing Elliott Currie, Angela Davis denounces the institutionalized racism and rampant capitalism that led to society's reliance on prisons: "The prison has become a looming presence in our society to an extent unparalleled in our history or that of any other industrial democracy. Short of major wars, mass incarceration has been the most thoroughly implemented government social program of our time."[31] This looming presence is one that most of us willfully ignore. To be clear, the term *prison-industrial complex* refers to the system of mass incarceration and the companies that benefit from prisons. The problem of the prison industrial complex—when companies profit from mass incarceration and are therefore invested in maintaining the system—stems from what King refers to as the three-headed monster of racism, militarism, and poverty that undergirds the proliferation of injustice in the United States.

Currently, the prison population of the United States totals over two million people, the largest prison population in the world. Most of these incarcerated people are Black, Brown, and poor. Mass incarceration is one of the most sinister motors of injustice in the twenty-first century. Angela Davis exposes the racist and sexist origins of prisons and the long struggle to dismantle them. Asking us to summon our imaginations to see a world without prisons, she notes that, if racist institutions like slavery and Jim Crow have been abolished, it is also possible to eradicate prisons. She argues that "the most difficult and urgent challenge today is that of creatively exploring new terrains of justice, where the prison no longer serves as our major anchor."[32] Furthermore, the grip of mass incarceration is not limited to the private and public prisons themselves, because, as Davis points out, "the reach of the prison-industrial complex is far beyond the prisons."[33] From education to immigration, the prison-industrial complex is militarizing institutions in the United States.

---

[31]Elliot Currie, cited in Davis, *Are Prisons Obsolete?*, 11.
[32]Davis, *Are Prisons Obsolete?*, 12.
[33]Davis, *Freedom Is a Constant Struggle*, 57.

King's critique that the United States was dithering in a culture of excess preventing the elimination of poverty captures succinctly the need for prison abolition: "A nation that continues year after year to spend more money on military defense than on programs of social uplift is approaching spiritual doom."[34] The same can be said of a nation that invests more on mass incarceration and police than on education. The amount of money that the United States allots to the prison-industrial complex is staggering. A nation that year after year continues to spend billions of dollars on mass incarceration is approaching moral and spiritual doom. The movement to abolish prisons and defund the police is born of a similar logic that King advanced in his antiwar speeches.

The New Jim Crow

Michelle Alexander's book *The New Jim Crow: Mass Incarceration in the Age of Colorblindness* explores how the creation of the prison-industrial complex is rooted in racism. In explaining mass incarceration as "the new Jim Crow," she returns to the birth of the penitentiary system in the United States. When it was published in 2010, the book popularized discussion of mass incarceration for the broader public and quickly became a *New York Times* best seller, making mainstream the terms *mass incarceration* and *prison-industrial complex*. Alexander's aptly dubbed reference to the new Jim Crow establishes a through line from slavery to Jim Crow to mass incarceration: "Like Jim Crow (and slavery), mass incarceration operates as a tightly networked system of laws, policies, customs, and institutions that operate collectively to ensure the subordinate status of a group defined largely by race."[35] An important part of her argument is that our current prison system is a direct outgrowth of chattel slavery. Furthermore, the title of Alexander's book implicitly invokes Martin Luther King Jr. through its reference to color blind-

---

[34]King, *Trumpet of Conscience*, 33.
[35]Alexander, *New Jim Crow,* 13.

ness, a concept that people frequently associate with the civil rights leader. She explains that we cannot isolate the problem of mass incarceration from the entire criminal justice system—the systems are insidiously yoked to one another. From policing to prisons, *The New Jim Crow* presents a legal and historical perspective on the criminal justice system. By unveiling how prisoners are treated like second-class citizens, Alexander unmasks a caste system that exists in our society.

A Political Crisis

It was over ten years ago when Michelle Alexander sounded a roaring alarm about mass incarceration: "a human rights nightmare is occurring on our watch. If we avert our gaze, history will judge us harshly."[36] Despite the wild popularity of her book, a decade after the publication of *The New Jim Crow*, it is clear that only minuscule inroads have been made into interrogating mass incarceration and advancing prison abolition. For example, Black people are six times more likely to be incarcerated than white people in the United States, transgender people of color represent the group most likely to be arrested and imprisoned, and women of color are the fastest-growing prison population. To this we can add the problem of police brutality, which is also linked to the prison-industrial complex. And as Keeanga-Yamahtta Taylor has persuasively argued, "The spectacle of unchecked police brutality and murder has morphed into a political crisis,"[37] yet it is a political crisis on which few politicians are commenting. As a result of the uprisings that emerged after George Floyd's killing in 2020, the United States is considering police reform bills for the first time. *The New Jim Crow* examines the phenomenon of mass incarceration and its implications for racial justice. It disabuses us of false notions of progress that accompany vacuous formations of "postracial America" and "color blindness."

---

[36]Alexander, *New Jim Crow,* 15.
[37]Keeanga-Yamahtta Taylor, *From #Blacklivesmatter to Black Liberation* (Chicago, IL: Haymarket Books, 2016), 4.

The book is a sobering study that exposes the caste system regulating society in the United States. As a "racialized system of control," the function of mass incarceration is to cast Black people separately.[38]

Ava DuVernay's documentary film *Thirteenth* continues along the same trajectory that Michelle Alexander, who is also one of the experts in the documentary, argues in *The New Jim Crow*. In *Thirteenth*, DuVernay examines the creation of prisons as a response to the Thirteenth Amendment and connects the history of slavery and its abolition to the rise of prisons. She reminds us that the prison system was built on slavery and remains tethered to it in pernicious ways. The Thirteenth Amendment gives freedom to people in the United States, prohibiting the existence of slavery, but it also states that only criminals are exempt from freedom. In other words, everybody is now free, except for criminals. A society that acted as though nobody's free until everybody's free would not have allowed this to happen. Consequently, the criminalization of Black people propelled the creation of the prison-industrial complex. The mass incarceration of Black and Brown people resulted in the startling statistic that the United States makes up only 5 percent of the world's population but houses 25 percent of the world's incarcerated people.

Like *The New Jim Crow*, *Thirteenth* achieved popular and mainstream success and, more importantly, extended the conversation about a failed system in which poor Black and Brown people are disproportionately represented in US prisons. It stitches together slavery, Jim Crow, the creation of the prison-industrial complex, and the beginnings of the Black Lives Matter movement. By exposing how the private prison industry has been shored up by organizations like the American Legislative Exchange Council (ALEC), a body with a financial interest in the prison business, the film takes a multilayered approach to showing how the prison system is able to be maintained. Notwithstanding the mainstream popularity of both

---

[38]Alexander, *New Jim Crow*, 14.

The New Jim Crow and *Thirteenth*, they fell short of calling for a revolution of values through prison abolition.

A REVOLUTION OF VALUES

Angela Davis, Ruth Wilson Gilmore, and Mariame Kaba are all examples of twenty-first-century social justice warriors who are sounding a trumpet of conscience around prison abolition. Their antiprison activism and writing demonstrate the ongoing need for transformation in our sick society. By bringing this work to a mainstream audience, Michelle Alexander, Ava DuVernay, and Bryan Stevenson have also intervened to transform people's minds and hearts toward justice. Nevertheless, despite the popularity of films and books about the injustice of our prison and punishment systems, the public conversation continues to center largely on reform and not on abolition. A true revolution of values is required if the movement for prison abolition is to spread beyond activists and academics. Clearly, their work on mass incarceration recalls King's radical and revolutionary vision. King was unequivocal in his belief that "the white power structure is seeking to keep the walls of segregation and inequality intact."[39] The prison-industrial complex is but one further example of how the white power structure maintains this wall of racist segregation, inequality, and oppression. All of these forms of oppression stem from the existence of white supremacy. As Mariame Kaba convincingly argues, "White supremacy does not thrive in spite of the menacing infrastructure of US criminalization and militarism—it thrives because of it."[40] From a faith perspective, it is concerning and seems antithetical to the gospel how rarely the church embraces the cause of prison abolition. Too often, the topic of prison abolition is met with the questions: What will happen to

---

[39]King, *Trumpet of Conscience*, 9.
[40]Mariame Kaba, *We Do This 'til We Free Us: Abolitionist Organizing and Transforming Justice* (Chicago: Haymarket, 2021), xvii.

the criminals? Where will they go? A justice-oriented view cannot merely be concerned with punishment.

Prison abolition requires what King called "a revolution of values." Today, people misunderstand the purpose and function of prisons. In the movement for prison abolition, Davis, Gilmore, and Kaba are not calling for something radically different from what King proposed. In fact, the prison abolition movement is one of the purest manifestations of a revolution of values unfolding today. As a revolution of values, prison abolition relies on restorative justice and reconciliation. As King implores, "We as a nation must undergo a true revolution of values," because "a true revolution of values will soon cause us to question the fairness and justice of many of our past and present policies. A true revolution of values will soon look uneasily on the glaring contrast between poverty and wealth,"[41] because the problem of mass incarceration perpetuates the disenfranchisement of the poor.

Building Life and Healing

King also notes that "a true revolution of values will lay hands on the world order and say of war: 'this way of settling differences is not just.'"[42] Using prisons to settle differences is not just. In many ways, mass incarceration replicates the values of the American war machine that King regularly indicted. First, we must recall what prison abolition actually means. Gilmore offers the simplest definition: "Abolition is about presence, not absence. It's about building life-affirming institutions. . . . Abolition has to be green, and in order to be green, it has to be red (anti-capitalist), and in order to be red, it has to be international."[43] Standing in contrast to this life-affirming presence that Gilmore avows, mass incarceration breeds death and

---

[41]King, *Trumpet of Conscience*, 32–33.

[42]King, *Trumpet of Conscience*, 33.

[43]Ruth Wilson Gilmore, "Making and Unmaking Mass Incarceration (MUMI)," keynote conversation between Ruth Wilson Gilmore, Mariame Kaba, and James Kilgore, Oxford, Mississippi, December 4, 2019.

destruction. As Angela Davis contends, "Jails and prisons are designed to break human beings, to convert the population into specimens in a zoo—obedient to our keepers, but dangerous to others."[44]

There is a healing element present when we consider the last part of King's statement that "a true revolution of values will lay hands on the world." The laying on of hands refers to a spiritual action. It also recalls the final scene in Ntozake Shange's play *For Colored Girls Who Have Considered Suicide / When the Rainbow Is Enuf*, when "a laying on of hands" transforms from the religious into the spiritual realm in order for Black women to know the healing power contained in their hands and their hearts. The world is in need of that kind of healing. Only with compassion and love will we be able to remember those who are in chains as though their chains are our own.

Prison abolition means ending a system that has been instrumental in perpetuating racism and poverty. As King notes, "The United States is substantially challenged to demonstrate that it can abolish not only the evils of racism but the scourge of poverty of whites as well as Negroes, and the horrors of war that transcend national borders and involve all mankind."[45] He often discussed the intersection of racism, poverty, and war. The combination of these three issues today manifests at every level of our society: we witness the lack of equity in our schools and health-care system, and we see money poured into policing and prisons instead of our communities and schools where they could be invested in children. As these problems unfold and persist, we see the prison-industrial complex's debilitating effects on Black and Brown people in society.

The Greatest Purveyor of Violence

Today, progressive activists, academics, and organizers denounce the use of violence to advance the reach of US power in the world, an advance that can also be understood as a new form of imperialism

---

[44]Davis, *Are Prisons Obsolete?*, 20.
[45]King, *Trumpet of Conscience*, 18.

or empire building. This is a position that King elaborated toward the end of his life: "I could never again raise my voice against the violence of the oppressed in the ghettos without having first spoken clearly to the greatest purveyor of violence in the world today: my own government."[46]

King's scathing critique of the United States as one of the world's greatest purveyors of violence remains true today. We see it in the unequivocal support of Israel, and the wars in Iraq and Afghanistan. King's international condemnation of violence allowed him to see the hypocrisy at home in the United States, where he was lauded for embracing nonviolence—a hypocrisy that is reflected today in the problem of mass incarceration and the proliferation of Black and Brown people in the prison-industrial complex. King's approach to justice was neither timid nor simple; it was radical and audacious. As Harding explains, "Apparently the love of God and neighbor . . . required nonconformity, conflict, and confrontation."[47] That perspective is far from peace-loving and genteel. It inspires us to be disruptive and to look for examples of our faith as a source of disruption.

More than half a century ago, King observed that "it is now incontestable that the wealth and the resources of the United States make the elimination of poverty perfectly practicable."[48] This is even more relevant today when the wealth gap has become especially outrageous. The year that Martin Luther King alongside many others began the movement that would become the Poor People's Campaign was also the last year of his life. It began with the Poor People's March on Washington—an economic justice movement intended to eliminate poverty. In the 1960s, King saw the end of poverty as a plausible goal based on the statistics on wealth in the United States. This goal is even more plausible today. Economic justice was central to King's vision for the world. The Poor People's

---

[46]King, *Trumpet of Conscience*, 24. See also Martin Luther King Jr., "Beyond Vietnam," April 4, 1967, NNRC (Riverside Church Archives), https://kinginstitute. stanford.edu.

[47]Harding, *Martin Luther King*, 17.

[48]King, *Trumpet of Conscience*, 15.

March did not take place until after his death, when it was organized by the Southern Christian Leadership Conference (SCLC) under the leadership of Ralph Abernathy. For over a month—May 12 to June 24, 1968—people occupied the Washington Mall to express their solidarity with the poor and demand policy changes around economic justice. The Poor People's Campaign sought to address poverty by bridging gaps of income and housing. The campaign also asked for "a revolution of values."

Mass incarceration is also an issue of economic justice. Poverty is catastrophically linked to the issue of mass incarceration because the majority of people who go to prison are there because they come from a lower socioeconomic background. In fact, people of means rarely face prison sentences at the same rate as poor people—especially for people on death row, as Bryan Stevenson makes clear in *Just Mercy*. Much work is needed to make economic justice a priority and a reality in the United States. Currently, neither is true. The work that the original Poor People's Campaign began in 1968 is the inspiration and has its modern configuration in Rev. Dr. William Barber's Poor People's Campaign: A National Call for Moral Revival, whose mission is to end poverty in the United States. But it has not yet reached the ubiquity of a mass movement.

King also rightfully critiqued how often commissions are created but no policies follow. "It was the same story with voting rights. The Civil Rights Commission, three years before we went to Selma, had recommended the changes we started marching for, but nothing was done until, in 1965, we created a crisis the nation couldn't ignore."[49] I have encountered a similar tendency while working toward anti-racist education in my children's schools. The superintendent's first response to our concerns was to create a task force and invite my spouse and me to join it. We were adamant in our position that a task force was not the answer to the problems we had in our town. Universities operate in a similar fashion. When King took a bold stance against the war in Vietnam, he did so because he felt obliged by his conscience: "I find myself obliged by conscience to end

---

[49]King, *Trumpet of Conscience*, 56.

my silence and to take a public stand against my country's war in Vietnam."[50] What if our approach to incarcerated people were the same as King's approach to the war in Vietnam? What if we choose to speak for—as well as with and alongside—incarcerated people as though they were in fact our brothers and sisters, taking seriously King's mandate that "we must speak for them, and raise the questions they cannot raise. These, too, are our brothers."[51] Taking such a stance requires an ethic that takes a stance against all oppressive systems, not only those that affect us personally.

Ending the Madness

Remembering King's words that "this is a sick society," and considering the year of 2020, when a global pandemic gripped the entire world, I could not end this chapter without addressing how COVID-19 has amplified and exacerbated the problem of mass incarceration. In our sick society, mass incarceration has accelerated the spread of the pandemic.[52] The deplorable conditions inside correctional institutions across the United States with their overcrowding, poor facilities, and close contact make for a perfect storm of widespread contagion. It is a painful reminder that federal government attention to the pandemic has been shaped by who is getting sick. As we saw with how the pandemic is affecting Black and Brown communities, the circumstances that led to this situation are far from new. Unsurprisingly, our disregard for the incarcerated population has led to the astonishing numbers of coronavirus deaths in US prisons, amplifying the injustice of a broken and depraved system.

The most recent edition of *The Trumpet of Conscience* published by Beacon Press has the subtitle "Dr. King's Final Testament on Racism, Poverty, and War." When we understand the prison-industrial complex as a product of "racism, poverty, and war," its utility as a

---

[50]King, *Trumpet of Conscience*, 21.

[51]King, *Trumpet of Conscience*, 28.

[52]Gregory Hooks and Wendy Sawyer, "Mass Incarceration, COVID-19, and Community Spread," Prison Policy Initiative, December 2020, https://www.prisonpolicy.org.

tool of racial and economic oppression also explains the reluctance to abolish prisons. When we consider the relationship between the criminal justice system and people who are poor, Black, and Brown, the racism and economic injustice behind the policies that guide the system become increasingly clear. I am convinced that, moved by his faith, Martin Luther King would have been an advocate for prison abolition. As we noted, King himself was arrested and put in jail at least thirty times, where he was often beaten and mistreated. In 1963, it was from a cell that he famously wrote in his "Letter from a Birmingham Jail" that "injustice anywhere is a threat to justice everywhere." And of course, long before King, a Brown-skinned Jesus was wrongfully accused, incarcerated, and killed by the death penalty. While hanging from the cross, he spoke to a proven criminal and promised him eternity, showing concern for the value of a condemned man. Prison abolition is fundamentally grounded in the belief that every person has equal value and is deserving of dignity and the full expression of their humanity.

In *The Trumpet of Conscience*, King posits that "if the anger of the peoples of the world at injustice of things is to be channeled into a revolution of love and creativity, we must begin now to work, urgently, with all the peoples, to shape a new world."[53] Davis, Kaba, and Gilmore are examples of abolitionists who are builders in service of reshaping the world.

We have much to learn from the unwavering activism of prison abolitionists. They instruct us to look at justice more holistically, to activate our imaginations, to understand freedom as a praxis, to center those whom our society has deemed the very least of these, and to engage hope as a discipline. Although the mainstream media has only recently begun to pay attention to prison abolition, the women discussed in this chapter have been pursuing this work for decades. Even a cursory look at the problem of mass incarceration and the prison-industrial complex as it currently stands reveals that it is "a brutalized system of racialized oppression and control."[54] It

---

[53]King, *Trumpet of Conscience*, 51.
[54]Alexander, *New Jim Crow*, 59.

is a system embedded in racism, poverty, militarism, and material-ism—an interrelated and evil system as described by King.

Prison abolition imagines an end to the madness. It recognizes that the madness must stop and that our current course is actually unsustainable. "Somehow this madness must cease. We must stop now. I speak as a child of God and brother to the suffering poor of Vietnam."[55]

More than fifty years after the death of Martin Luther King Jr., we are still a country whose "proneness to injustice" should be disquieting.[56] We sit by quietly while children are separated from their families, then kept in cages; while an entire people are being swallowed up by prisons; while people are being raped on college campuses; and while people are dying because they do not have access to health care. The madness continues, but somehow it must cease. When we listen to the sound of the trumpet of conscience, we search for the tune that will begin the process of ceasing this madness. In the present state of our society, prison abolition appears to be a lofty goal. Sounding the trumpet of conscience requires that we unveil the injustice of mass incarceration and imagine a world in which prisons finally become obsolete. We must envision this world, because, as Mariame Kaba urges, "we must also fight for a vision of the world we want to inhabit."[57]

---

[55]King, *Trumpet of Conscience*, 31.

[56]Here I am purposefully echoing what King describes as "our proneness to adjust to injustice" (King, *Trumpet of Conscience*, 34).

[57]Mariame Kaba and Kelly Hayes, "A Jailbreak of the Imagination: Seeing Prisons for What They Are and Demanding Transformation," Truthout, May 3, 2018, https://truthout.org.

Making Justice Irresistible

You have to act as if it were possible to radically transform the world. And you have to do it all the time.

—Angela Davis

I began this book with King's provocative statement that we live in a sick society, and then I lamented that this continues to be true today. The exhausting longevity of white supremacy and hetero-patriarchy begs the questions: Will we win this fight? Will we be free? Or, to ask King's question, "Today the question is not whether we shall be free but by what course we will win?"[1] But what does winning look like? Does the language of winning accommodate what we know about power and oppression? What would a just world look like? What does true freedom look like? How do we create a more just world that looks like the one that we want to inhabit? I don't have the answers to these questions but, like King, I am hoping that we *will win* and that freedom will someday truly reign. At the same time, I understand and appreciate Coretta Scott King's insightful point that "struggle is a never-ending process. Freedom is never really won, you earn it and win it in every generation."

---

[1]King, *Trumpet of Conscience*, 4.

And, as Robin D. G. Kelley suggests, it is "a process that can and must transform us."

More than fifty years after King posed his own questions about winning in *The Trumpet of Conscience*, we have yet to chart the course to victory. The social justice movements that we have explored in this book—racial injustice, gender-based violence, and mass incarceration—are but three examples where our society needs desperately to listen for and to hear the trumpet of conscience. Our conscience asks that we be moved by compassion for people who suffer as a result of these forms of injustice. Our faith demands that we suffer with them as though we ourselves were suffering. In some ways, the course of justice has been mapped. The Movement for Black Lives (M4BL) puts forth very clearly concrete policies needed for Black and Brown people to experience freedom and justice. Antirape advocates like Tarana Burke champion the cause of empowerment through empathy, while others like Aishah Shahidah Simmons chart the course to restorative justice through "Love WITH Accountability." Prison abolitionists like Gilmore, Kaba, and Davis have delineated paths for building a world without prisons. By imagining otherwise, we can create the kind of world that we envision without sexual violence, without anti-Blackness, without prisons. To create this world is to create more justice.

Several years ago, I was on an academic panel when the scholar who spoke ahead of me, queer theorist Rinaldo Walcott, stated, "I always approach my work with the question, how do I create more justice?" That question has remained with me. What if we all approached our work and our lives with that same question? How do we create more justice? The question resonates with me as an educator, a parent, an activist, and a person of faith. When the Biden-Harris ticket succeeded in putting an end to the Trump presidency, many saw this moment as a sea change and the definitive end of Trumpism, which had cast a pall over the United States. We celebrated the victory of a ticket that includes Kamala Harris, the first woman vice president. Having the US vice president be a Black woman of South Asian and Jamaican heritage is also unprecedented and exciting. It felt like a collective sigh of relief and a wave of hope was washing over us. However, history cautions us to remember that justice and governance are discrete entities. The coronavirus continues to rage on. This public health crisis routinely reveals more than ever the extent to which we are a "sick society." The many social inequalities are being magnified and amplified. Undocumented people are more marginalized than ever as they are driven into hiding and fear for their safety. We are wise to recall King's words that "a social movement that only moves people is merely a revolt. A movement that changes both people and institutions is a revolution."[2] Our need for a revolutionary movement that transforms both people and institutions is pressing and urgent.

The great themes of social change and hope for the future that King espouses in *The Trumpet of Conscience* have much in common with movements for social justice today. While we have only focused on three social justice issues, there are many more to consider. King spoke extensively about economic injustice like income inequality. As he noted, "It is now incontestable that the wealth and resources of the United States make the elimination of poverty perfectly practicable,"[3] and this continues to be so five decades later.

Today our society is even more unequal than it was in the 1960s. In fact, over the past three decades the wealthiest 1 percent have doubled their wealth and control almost half of the country's financial resources. Since King's death, racist policies continue to be insidious and instrumental in legislating anti-Blackness. In a 1967 speech to the Southern Christian Leadership Conference in Atlanta, King laid out a pointed critique of white supremacy and institutional violence:

> It is incontestable and deplorable that Negroes have committed crimes, but they are derivative crimes. They are born of the greater crimes of white society. When we ask Negroes to abide

---

[2]Martin Luther King Jr., *Why We Can't Wait* (New York: Harper and Row, 1964).
[3]King, *Trumpet of Conscience*, 15.

by the law, let us also declare that the white man does not abide by law in the ghettos. . . . The slums are the handiwork of a vicious system of the white society; Negroes live in them but do not make them any more than a prisoner makes a prison.[4]

THE FUTURE

So where does the future point us today? What does our conscience oblige us to do?[5] When we listen for the trumpet call of conscience, what does it sound like and what does it tell us? I have a tendency to approach justice issues from the perspective of what is left out. In other words, what has been obscured, silenced, or unnamed in our current struggles? This approach, like that of Jesus, stems from the determination to make room for what is excluded and ignored.

As the child of Haitian immigrants, I was raised on the shining example of the Haitian Revolution as the ultimate freedom movement. This insurrection against slavery led to a true revolution of values, asserting that Black lives mattered more than the wealth derived from the plantocracy. I am also aware that my ancestors rose up and used violence to overthrow white supremacy. Nonviolence was not an option for them.

Now, I could have focused on many other topics in this book: environmental justice, the refugee crisis, the plight of our fellow undocumented Americans, ableism, or climate change. However, when we look at the end of King's life for instruction and see how he moved toward poverty as an issue and an antiwar position, we

---

[4]King, "Crisis in America's Cities." From the *Atlantic* article: "Three weeks after 43 people were killed in race riots in Detroit—the worst of the more than 150 urban riots during the 'long hot summer' of 1967—King addressed the Southern Christian Leadership Conference in Atlanta. He delineated the causes of the violence, notably 'the white backlash,' black unemployment, racial discrimination, and the war in Vietnam."

[5]Here I am purposefully using King's words in *Trumpet of Conscience* concerning the War in Vietnam: "I find myself obliged by conscience to end my silence" (21).

notice that, as Audre Lorde states, there is no such thing as single-issue struggles. All of these issues are intertwined. Today, therefore, King would stand with people who are undocumented because he said in 1967 when discussing the war in Vietnam, "We are called to speak for the weak, for the voiceless, for the victims of our nation, and for those it calls enemy, for no document from human hands can make these humans any less our brothers."[6] As someone who saw himself as a global citizen and lambasted the United States as "the greatest purveyor of violence in the world," he understood that documentation was but a cog in the system of uprooting our human citizenship.

Our contemporary celebrations and citations of Martin Luther King reveal that he is broadly underestimated and misunderstood. I often wonder why the people who laud King's colorblind positions never mention the many times that he spoke explicitly to and about white people. In *The Trumpet of Conscience*, he repeatedly condemns racist white people and describes the evils of white supremacy. In the essay "Impasse on Race Relations," he makes it clear that "it is not the race per se that we fight but the policies and ideology that leaders of that race have formulated to perpetuate oppression."[7] As King began to speak out more about the "terrible economic injustices," he did so not only because of his passionate heart for the poor but also because of his desire to see a more just world. He recognized the intrinsic link between peace and justice. As Vincent Harding notes, "For him, Americans could pursue effective peace only as we recognized how intrinsically it is joined to justice, especially justice in the uses and distribution of the world's common resources."[8]

What does it mean to create more justice, if not to enable every person to live in dignity and with decency? A world in which all can flourish. The world that King lived in was so far from this reality, and I fear that in many ways we are even farther from it

---

[6] King, *Trumpet of Conscience*, 25.
[7] King, *Trumpet of Conscience*, 9.
[8] Harding, *Martin Luther King*, 13.

today. Grieving the leadership of the government infected by white supremacy in the 1960s, King denounced the leaders who refused to stand against racial and economic injustices. King deplored unequivocally the inaction of the leadership: "If we do not act, we shall surely be dragged down the long, dark, and shameful corridors of time reserved for those who possess power without compassion, might without morality, and strength without sight."[9] These are strong words from the person whose primary focus was to love his neighbor and turn the other cheek, and they prod us to ponder King's main concerns: power dynamics and power relations. Critiquing circuits of power and how they maintain injustice demands that we not only think about race but also about gender, sexuality, class, ableism, and other forms of marginalization. Power dynamics were also one of the preferred subjects of Jesus Christ, who came to turn power structures on their head.

The critique of extant power structures punctuates King's social commentary and sermons with precision and conviction. The "long, dark, shameful corridor" refers to people in leadership for whom power and strength are their only concerns. Take, for example, how King rarely mentioned white supremacy by name but was clearly aware of how it operated and the need to upend it. When he uses the term *white man*, he explains that his goal is not to generalize about individual white people, but rather to indicate how white supremacy as a structure relies on racism to operate and proliferate:

> In using the term "white man" I am seeking to describe in general terms the Negro's adversary. It is not meant to encompass all white people. There are millions who have morally risen above prevailing prejudices.[10]

This view resonates with what Ibram X. Kendi calls the antiracist struggle, where the goal is to fight the policies. He writes in *How*

---

[9]King, *Trumpet of Conscience*, 34.
[10]King, *Trumpet of Conscience*, 9.

to Be Anti-Racist that a racist upholds and advances racist policies whereas an antiracist works to dismantle them. Martin Luther King was a strident critic of white supremacy and often discussed whiteness as a purveyor of injustice.

A VOICE FOR THE VOICELESS

King's vision is not so distant from many of the activists and thinkers fighting injustice today, whether they be the leaders of the Black Lives Matter movement, anti-rape advocates, or prison abolitionists. When we read *The Trumpet of Conscience* and focus on the more radical parts of his vision, the relevance of King's message still resonates today.

The fact that there is still a clean water crisis happening in Flint, Michigan, would unquestionably agitate King, who decried the conditions of life in poor and predominately Black cities: "A complex of causes are found in the degenerating conditions of urban life. The cities are gasping in polluted air and enduring contaminated water."[11] In Nigeria, #EndSARS is an example of militarism abroad that requires international outcry. And just as he took an unpopular stance against the Vietnam War because his conscience inspired him to do so, I imagine that King would have supported the movement for Palestinian liberation.

The Trumpet of Conscience also shows that King was not always hopeful or optimistic about the road ahead. He spoke the language of lament as fluently as he preached with a prophetic voice: "The elements of social catastrophe have accumulated in such vast array that no remedies may be available."[12] The fear that there may be no remedies available remains with us today, even in the face of what some have deemed as impressive progress to advance racial justice. What does the quest for life, freedom, and justice look like

---

[11]King, *Trumpet of Conscience*, 12.
[12]King, *Trumpet of Conscience*, 13.

for a rape survivor? What does it look like for someone who has been so wounded by domestic violence and transphobic violence that they are homeless and isolated? Are we aware that we live in a world where so many people are suffering from causes that we could root out if we were truly committed to pursuing justice? If we are, then where is our moral outrage? Why do we not throw open the doors of our churches to meaningfully embrace those who are most marginalized? Why do we remain silent in the face of a health system so cruel that people die unnecessarily and are locked out of care? On the one hand, there is a fire raging right now against the rampant racism and racial injustice of this country that allowed the murders of George Floyd and Breonna Taylor to happen.[13] But on the other hand, why has it taken so long, and where will this reignited activism lead us to?

Martin Luther King's advocacy against the war in Vietnam reveals that he saw himself as a "voice for the voiceless."[14] His concern was not only for the people of Vietnam but also for the US troops who were fighting the war, many of whom were already plagued by the problem of racism at home. His position against the war is instructive insofar as it illuminates King's global vision. It shows that when he used the term *brother* or *sister*," he extended that fellowship not only to those who looked like him or lived in the same country. Much has been written about King's global vision and how a trip to India inspired him to look at the world through international eyes and to see himself as a citizen of the world: "I speak as a citizen of the world, for the world as it stands aghast at the path we have taken."[15] While Martin Luther King, for many, is the template for what a Black freedom movement should look like, many leaders and activists have come after him and improved on his vision.

---

[13] King, *Trumpet of Conscience*, 55: "There is a fire raging now among the Negroes and the poor of this country."

[14] I am referring to when King writes, "I have tried to give a voice to the voiceless in Vietnam," King, *Trumpet of Conscience*, 30.

[15] King, *Trumpet of Conscience*, 31.

One of my former pastors was committed to debunking colloquial Christian terms. He often told us that ministry is just service. While the church liked to mystify the meaning of ministry and make it into something more elaborate and complex, he demystified it and so many other words that were born out of our Christian vocabulary. For King, it was also clear that ministry was about serving as Jesus did, which is why he wrote so frequently about commitment to the relationship of this ministry to the making of peace, and why he was determined to address the "beloved community."[16]

King's "A Christmas Sermon on Peace," which he delivered in 1967, described an atmosphere similar to what we lived through in 2020. "Everywhere paralyzing fears harrow people by day and haunt them by night."[17] For many today, these fears are surfacing as a result of the pandemic, while for others there is a fatigue around racism as we wonder whether there will ever be any respite from racial violence and terror. As some have noted, we are living through two pandemics: one is a public health crisis; the other is a result of systemic racism in this country. *The Trumpet of Conscience* confirms how the march by twenty-first-century movements toward justice is not a far cry from what one of the most lauded and cited Black freedom fighters envisioned. It asks us to consider our brothers and sisters not only in this country but throughout the world. "We must speak for them, and raise the questions they cannot raise. These, too, are our brothers."[18] In addition, we need not only "speak for" but also allow ourselves to be "spoken for." In other words, we must practice solidarity and ascertain how it is not only mutually beneficial but necessary.

In this Christmas sermon from *The Trumpet of Conscience*, King describes the three different kinds of love in the Christian tradition: *eros*, *philos*, and *agape*. These three distinct manifestations of love are well known in the church. If King returns to the three words for love in the Greek as a way to explain why love is needed, the

---

[16]King, *Trumpet of Conscience*, 25.
[17]King, *Trumpet of Conscience*, 69.
[18]King, *Trumpet of Conscience*, 28.

reason is because the return to love is most essential and necessary to his vision. King urged those around him to look to Jesus as the model in order to truly know and walk in the way of love. As King highlights, "Jesus reminds us that love is greater than liking. Love is understanding, creative redemptive goodwill toward all. And I think this is where we are, as a people, in our struggle for racial justice."[19] For King, this power shined brighter than the sun, illuminating every quest for justice. Notwithstanding the importance of love, and despite what many like to remember about his vision, he also made clear that loving one's enemies is an arduous task.

A DREAM OR NIGHTMARE

"I had had, and must confess to you today that not long after talking about that dream, I started seeing it turn into a nightmare."[20] King references his dream turning into a nightmare more than once in *The Trumpet of Conscience,* signaling to us that this thought weighed heavily on his mind. As he continues, the idea of a dream deferred becomes even more searing. "Yes, I am personally the victim of deferred dreams, of blasted hopes, but in spite of that I close today by saying that I still have a dream, because, you know, you can't give up in life. If you lose hope, somehow you lose that vitality that keeps life moving, you lose that courage to be, that quality that helps you to go on in spite of all. And so today I still have a dream."[21] What are these deferred dreams and blasted hopes to which King is referring? How does his understanding of what he has lost or of his disappointments resonate with us today? His words recall Langston Hughes's poem "Harlem,"[22] in which the poet famously asks, "What

---

[19]King, *Trumpet of Conscience*, 76.
[20]King, *Trumpet of Conscience*, 78.
[21]King, *Trumpet of Conscience*, 79.
[22]Langston Hughes, "Harlem," from *The Collected Works of Langston Hughes*. Copyright © 2002 by Langston Hughes. Reprinted by permission of Harold Ober Associates Inc.

happens to a dream deferred?" and ends with "*Or does it explode?*" The careful reader understands that King's answer would be similar to that of the poet—a dream deferred explodes, and the debris scatters throughout our broken world.

HOPE, DREAM, AND FIGHT

In the conclusion to the final lecture in *The Trumpet of Conscience*, King urges the reader to "bring new light to the dark chambers of pessimism."[23] Today, the dark chambers of pessimism do indeed threaten to engulf us. The reality that we are living in two pandemics returns us to the quotation with which I began this book: "This is a sick society." The evils of racism, militarism, and materialism continue to impact the trajectory of our society, making real freedom feel elusive at best, and at worst, impossible. Anti-Black racism, gender-based violence, and mass incarceration are unrelenting forms of injustice facing us in this moment. Peace and justice feel obscurely distant today. Another King statement so often cited that it has become almost a platitude professes, "We shall overcome because the arc of the moral universe is long but it bends toward justice."[24] But today it does not always feel like the arc of the moral universe is bending toward justice. As Black people are killed by police, or die because of inadequate health care, or are put in prisons to feed the system of mass incarceration, and more survivors of rape are categorically not believed, justice feels elusive and, at times, entirely unattainable. There is little evidence that police will stop killing Black people, that Black women and girls will be remembered as much as Black men and boys are, that poverty will be eradicated, that we will live in a world free of sexual violence, and that human rights for all will be universally

---

[23]King, *Trumpet of Conscience*, 80.

[24]John Craig, "Wesleyan Baccalaureate Is Delivered by Dr. King," *Hartford Courant*, June 8, 1964. In 1964 King delivered the Baccalaureate sermon at the commencement exercises for Wesleyan University in Middletown, Connecticut.

valued. Wars continue to threaten the livelihood of people all over the world—from Syria to Sudan, the Democratic Republic of the Congo, and Ethiopia. From the political unrest percolating in Haiti to the lack of attention to three hundred girls kidnapped in Nigeria, human rights abuses around the world impel us to recognize that injustice is everywhere. There is very little to suggest that the world we dream of realizing will ever be made possible.

Yet we hope, we dream, and we fight. And we do so with joy because we know that there is beauty in the struggle. The dark chambers of pessimism that threaten to engulf us are dangerous because they want not only to chisel away at our hope, they threaten to swallow it whole. And to quote Bryan Stevenson again, "Hopelessness is the enemy of justice." In other words, as soon as we lose hope, we begin to lose our will and desire to fight. We begin to believe that we cannot surmount the challenges of this world and this century. When we struggle for justice without hope, the fight overwhelms us. We forget to persevere and neglect to look at history and recall all of those who did, so that we can be here. We do not look to the future and remember what we are fighting for. Even when we look around us and see little evidence that the arc does indeed bend toward justice, as King reminds us, losing hope will only make failure certain. What Ashon Crawley calls "imagining otherwise" is an expression that captures the need for hope. Imagining otherwise means not only seeing what is directly in front of us, it asks that we go further by engaging our imaginations and dwelling on the visions they reveal. As Mariame Kaba encourages us, "Hope is a discipline [and] we have to practice it every single day."[25]

Many people believe that, if he were alive today, Martin Luther King would be proud of the progress made in this country because today little Black girls and boys can sit down with little white girls and boys in schools, on buses, and in public. I am not so sure of such monumental progress and believe that it is a myth. It is a myth because the majority of Black people in this country continue to suf-

---

[25]Kaba, *We Do This 'til They Free Us,* 27.

fer from mass incarceration, unemployment and underemployment, health-care disparities, and other forms of institutionalized injustice. I agree, rather, with Austin Channing Brown, who writes, "I hope there is progress I can sincerely applaud on the horizon. Because the extrajudicial killing of Black people is still too familiar. Because the racist rhetoric that Black people are lazier, more criminal, more undeserving than white people is still too familiar. Because the locking up of a disproportionate number of Black bodies is still too familiar. Because the beating of Black people in the streets is still too familiar. History is collapsing on itself once again."[26] I too hope for actual progress, for real freedom, and for true justice someday to be a reality and not a dream.

THE CALL TO CONSCIENCE

If we follow the clarion call of the trumpet of conscience, then we know and understand that there is much work to be done. Being led by conscience means taking unfavorable stances. The call to conscience is a call to action. When King took his unpopular stance against the Vietnam War, he said that he felt obliged by conscience to do so: "I find myself obliged by conscience to end my silence and to take a public stand against my country's war in Vietnam."[27] What does our conscience call us to do? Similarly, in a letter written in 1967, the Russian novelist and Nobel Laureate Aleksandr Solzhenitsyn persuasively connected justice and conscience: "Justice is conscience, not a personal conscience but the conscience of the whole of humanity. Those who clearly recognize the voice of their own conscience usually recognize also the voice of justice." The voice of our own conscience calls us toward justice. We are to listen to ourselves, to our hearts. If we are to look for and listen to the way of love and seriously embrace the idea that justice is what

[26]Brown, *I'm Still Here*, 152.
[27]King, *Trumpet of Conscience*, 21.

love looks like in public, then we must not only *work* together but *walk* together.

In reading this book, perhaps you were looking to reconnect with King's vision and mission in order to find hope for the twenty-first century. Perhaps you too were tired of the "boxed-in" King and searching for a more nuanced and personal exploration of his legacy. To my Black brothers and sisters who came to this book longing for the King legacy and looking to imagine a different way forward and to those who are tired of watching images of Black people being killed by police, of Black people saying, "I can't breathe," I ask that you please pause and take a breath. Breath is precious and sacred. We need you to breathe. Your breath is life. Take time to breathe. Being Black is not what drains us. White supremacy and anti-Blackness drain us. Being Black is a joy and a gift. Let us continue to love each other, and love ourselves, and celebrate all that is beautiful, joyful, and sacred about our people. And take time to feel, "to feel your feelings," because that is where we can discern where our conscience is moving us.

The revolution of values, love, and creativity that we organize in this century must be the collective responsibility of anyone who cares about justice, but it requires systemic change. To suffer with those who are suffering as though we ourselves are suffering requires that we participate in the movement not because it affects us personally but because we understand that lives and human rights are at stake. I am not sure that any justice issue can be resolved without a communal, collective, and collaborative approach. As the Haitian proverb says, "Men anpil chay pa lou" (With many hands, the load is made light). We must lighten the load because the burden of this work is heavy. The emotional labor of our contemporary justice movement weighs on our hearts and minds even as we do the work. Alice Walker famously wrote, "Resistance is the secret of joy."[28] By finding joy in the resistance, we locate our justice work in something larger than ourselves. God girds us for this work.

---

[28] Alice Walker, *Possessing the Secret of Joy* (New York: New Press, 2008), 281.

During the past year, I have experienced rage, anguish, despair, frustration, sadness, fear, hopelessness, renewed faith, confusion, desperation, and resolve—yet none of these emotions feel contradictory. As human beings, we are amazing in our ability to feel and to hold contradictory thoughts. Like every Black parent, I fear for my children—both my sons *and* my daughters—knowing that they will inevitably experience racist abuse in their lives. I wonder how it will manifest. I hope and pray that it will not be fatal. But in the Black community where we operate according to the ethos of the village, I know that the loss of any Black life strikes each of us in the heart. Even when my children are still alive, we feel the loss of other Black children. Our feelings are both/and. So I can be disturbed by how my children are minoritized in our town, even while I am encouraged by the friends and neighbors for whom I know Black lives actually do matter: friends like those not only send messages of love and solidarity but also back up those gestures with genuine action; friends who not only acknowledge their privilege, but also spend it by publicly taking a stance against racism; friends who do more than talk the talk. What does it mean to begin our justice work from a place of love and humility? What does it look like to allow conscience to be the animating force behind our quest for justice?

A BELOVED COMMUNITY

What does a "beloved community" mean today? For me, it is a community where people are more than just allies. Educate yourselves and your children, demand justice, fight for the friends and neighbors you say you value. As we noted earlier in the book, in "I've Been to the Mountaintop," King retells the story of the Samaritan on the road, and ends by suggesting that whereas those who refused to stop along the way for the wounded man on the road ask, "If I stop to help this man, what will happen to me?" the Good Samaritan reverses the question: "If I do not stop to help this man, what will happen to him?" That's the question we need to ask ourselves today. "If I do not stop to help—demand justice, advocate, empathize, and love anyone on the margins in our community, what will happen to them?"

I want white people to understand that being an ally requires more of us than hashtag activism. The goal must be to be more than an ally because allies align with a cause from a distance. You must all follow through with action. White supremacy cannot be dismantled without *your* labor; it is not for Black people alone to carry. Together we can demand systemic change.

Martin Luther King understood the call to be a loving neighbor, so much so that he moved to one of Chicago's most impoverished neighborhoods toward the end of his life. As Vincent Harding explains, he did so because he recognized that "his love of neighbor demanded that he be neighbor, that he insert his life into the condition of his neighbor, that he challenge . . . the whole structure of Jericho Road, that he do it with his total being."[29] The historic struggle for social justice in the United States demonstrates that our common humanity is constantly under threat.

When we remember Sandra Bland, Rekia Boyd, Philando Castile, Trayvon Martin, Tony McDade, Michael Brown, Eric Garner, Breonna Taylor, Ahmaud Arbery, and George Floyd, we must remember their lives, not only their deaths. We must remember that, before their deaths were caught on camera, they lived full abundant lives. We heard about them because of their deaths—and their deaths must certainly enrage us—but we should care about them because of their lives. That is what Black Lives Matter means. Black lives matter beyond the pale of death. And so,

We speak their names;
We mourn their deaths;
We rage at the injustice of their murders;
We pray for their families;

---

[29]Harding, *Martin Luther King*, 11.

We honor their spirits;
We lament the loss of their lives; and
We remember their words.

As a Black mother, a professor, a feminist, a wife, and a follower of Jesus, I wrestle with all of these feelings. My God instructs me to do justice, to love mercy, and to walk humbly. But I find it hard to breathe, and I am still . . . so . . . tired.

It was in 1964 that the inimitable civil rights activist Fannie Lou Hamer declared, "I am sick and tired of being sick and tired." Years later, we are *still* sick and tired of being sick and tired. If we are to learn from *The Trumpet of Conscience*, we must heed the instruction to imagine and develop new strategies of resistance. The both/and helps me to feel my feelings. We are tired *and* we continue to fight; we believe because faith is being sure of what you hope for and certain of what you do not see. We hurt from the pain in the present, and imagine better futures. We counter our feelings of hopelessness by practicing hope as a discipline. We do not see justice, and we will not stop working for it to come. We do so because our ancestors did the same for us. They fought, and in my case as a woman of Haitian descent, set an island aflame, so that they could have freedom. To honor their legacy we must remember, we must fight, we must protest and pray, we must organize and mobilize, and we must work and believe, even as we cry in anguish and despair. In a series of parables on the kingdom of God, Jesus tells us that the work of justice is to focus on the overlooked: "'I'm telling the solemn truth: Whenever you did one of these things to someone overlooked or ignored, that was me—you did it to me'" (Matt 25:40 MSG).

As Harding notes, "We are called to speak for the weak, for the voiceless, for the victims of our nation and for those it calls enemy; for no document from human hands can make these humans any less our brother."[30] Our God calls us not only to serve the least of these, but to be proximate to them, to walk alongside them and be

---

[30]Harding, *Martin Luther King*, 15.

in community with them in ways that push past symbolism. Martin Luther King lived by this command, and any of us who care about justice should do so as well.

But how do we respond to the fact that, for King, women are considered the least of these and that he not only barely paid attention to them, he also exploited them? How do we make sense of this? What's missing here is how King failed to reconcile gender justice with the issues that were close to him. Today, it is impossible to consider racial justice from a narrow perspective that does not include gender, sexuality, and class. In fact, this resonates well with Lisa Sharon Harper's observation that God must be a Black woman because, when we think of the marginalized people in society, Black women are the face at the bottom of the well.

THE WAY FORWARD

The way forward takes the past into account, imagines a different future, and encourages us to build a better world. With *The Trumpet of Conscience* as our guide, we have been in search of wisdom and insight into our current moment and three movements representing the most pressing social justice issues of our time. These movements—whether they begin with love like the Black Lives Matter movement, a call for empowerment through empathy like the Me Too movement, or foreground global interconnectedness like prison abolition—are not at the remove of the struggle for Black freedom. We need the Holy Spirit; we need the spirit to guide us, to lead us, and to fill us as we move toward the goal of freedom. King not only understood this but lived it. When he speaks of conscience and asks that we allow our conscience to move us to act, he is also referring to the nudges and the prodding of the Holy Spirit. The Spirit allows, opens, and animates our minds to imagine otherwise and to do the work of justice by stretching our imaginations. The work of conscience is the work of the Spirit. Going back to the words of Aleksandr Solzhenitsyn regarding the relationship between justice and conscience, a faith-based justice is informed by a knowledge of God, accompanied by the presence of God, and led by the discernment of the Spirit. It is the same spirit described by M. Shawn Copeland, who in 2020 captured the anguish in response to the anti-Black violence that erupted:

> During these soul-wrenching days, we do well to remember that the Spirit cannot and will not be made captive, that the Spirit will not and cannot be tamed. Just as wind blows where and when it wills, so too does Spirit-*ruah*. The Spirit animates dissent and protest against any and all refusals to acknowledge and revere the presence of the divine in each and every human being, against any and all who stifle the breathing of others. The Spirit gifts those who grieve and hurt with comfort and consolation, those who strategize and plan with understanding and wisdom, those who march and stand and kneel with fortitude and courage.[31]

As noted at the beginning, this is not a book about Martin Luther King, but rather a book about social justice movements. It is a book that meditates on how King's vision at the end of his life can serve us today as we confront urgent problems such as the continued quest for racial justice, the problem of gender injustice, and the egregious phenomenon of mass incarceration. But this book also asks us not only to listen for the trumpet of conscience but also to feel the wind of the spirit as we discern and interrogate our own conscience. We need to think together about how to create more justice and how to work toward it with faith so that we leave no one behind and invite everyone to the table. We have such a long way to go, and we must all join King in saying that the madness continues—and it must stop.[32] Perhaps listening for the trumpet of conscience and heed-

---

[31]Copeland, "Breath & Fire."

[32]King, *Trumpet of Conscience*, 31: "Somehow this madness must cease. We must stop now. I speak as a child of God."

ing its call is no more than this. Armed with discernment breathed by the Spirit, holding onto hope, and guided by our faith that does justice, we work for freedom, believing and imagining its myriad possibilities. And we do this, "until we free us" because until all of us are free, none of us are.[33]

---

[33]Here I am purposefully invoking both Mariame Kaba and Fannie Lou Hamer.

Glossary

Black freedom movement: A distinct era in the African American struggle for civil and human rights that began in the mid-1940s and ended in the mid-1970s. It encompasses two of the most unique and enduring periods of Black activism: the civil rights movement and the Black Power movement.

Feminism: Belief in and advocacy of the political, economic, and social equality of the sexes.

Gender-based violence: Violence directed against a person because of their gender. Women and men experience gender-based violence, but the majority of victims are women and girls. This umbrella term includes intimate partner violence, sexual violence, street harassment, sexual abuse, and sexual harassment.

Intersectionality: A lens or prism for seeing how oppressions are linked. It refers to how marginalized identities compound and exacerbate one another.

Misogynoir: the term coined by Moya Bailey that means violence against, dislike of, contempt for, or ingrained prejudice against Black women.

Prison abolitionist movement: People committed to dismantling the prison industrial complex and building systems of rehabilitation that do not involve locking people away.

Prison-industrial complex: The profit-driven relationship that exists between the government and the corporations that build, supply, manage, and service prisons, contributing to increased prison rates for people who are marginalized.

Rape: The penetration of a bodily orifice (vagina, anus, or mouth) by another body part or an object against a person's will or without their consent.

Rape culture: A society or environment in which rape is prevalent and sexual violence is normalized by the media and popular culture, or through social norms; a complex set of beliefs that encourage male sexual aggression and support violence against women. In a rape culture, women perceive a continuum of threatened violence that ranges from sexual remarks to sexual touching to rape itself.

Restorative justice: practices that work to repair and prevent harm by addressing the needs of all involved in an incident, without calling on police or relying on punitive solutions.

Sexual violence: An umbrella term encompassing rape, sexual harassment, incest, sexual abuse, and street harassment.

Selected Bibliography

BOOKS

Abernathy, Ralph David. *And the Walls Came Tumbling Down: An Autobiography.* New York: HarperCollins, 1991.

Alexander, Michelle. *The New Jim Crow: Mass Incarceration in the Age of Colorblindness.* 10th ed. New York: New Press, 2020.

Baldwin, James. *The Fire Next Time.* New York: Vintage, 1994.

Baldwin, Lewis V. *There Is a Balm in Gilead: The Cultural Roots of Martin Luther King.* Minneapolis: Fortress Press, 1991.

Bambara, Toni Cade. "On the Issue of Roles." In *The Black Woman: An Anthology*, ed. Toni Cade Bambara. New York: Washington Square Press, 2005.

Brown, Austin Channing. *I'm Still Here: Black Dignity in a World Made for Whiteness.* New York: Convergent Books, 2018.

Buchwald, Emilie, Pamela Fletcher, and Martha Roth, eds. *Transforming a Rape Culture.* New York: Milkweed Editions, 1995.

Cone, James H. *Black Theology and Black Power.* Maryknoll, NY: Orbis Books, 2018.

———. *The Cross and the Lynching Tree.* Maryknoll, NY: Orbis Books, 2013.

———. *Said I Wasn't Gonna Tell Nobody: The Making of a Black Theologian.* Maryknoll, NY: Orbis Books, 2018.

Davis, Angela. *Are Prisons Obsolete?* New York: Seven Stories, 2003.

————. *Freedom Is a Constant Struggle: Ferguson, Palestine, and the Foundations of a Movement.* Chicago: Haymarket, 2016.

Dyson, Michael Eric. *I May Not Get There with You: The True Martin Luther King Jr.* New York: Free Press, 2001.

Edwards, Erica. *Charisma and the Fictions of Black Leadership.* Minneapolis: University of Minnesota Press, 2018.

Garza, Alicia. "Dear Mama Harriet." In *Radical Hope: Letters of Love and Dissent in Dangerous Times*, ed. Carolina de Robertis. New York: Vintage, 2017.

————. *The Purpose of Power: How We Come Together When We Fall Apart.* New York: Penguin Random House, 2020.

Gilmore, Ruth Wilson. *Golden Gulag: Prisons, Surplus, Crisis, and Opposition in Globalizing California.* Berkeley: University of California Press, 2007.

Harding, Vincent. *Martin Luther King: The Inconvenient Hero.* Rev. ed. Maryknoll, NY: Orbis Books, 2013.

Harper, Lisa Sharon. *The Very Good Gospel: How Everything Wrong Can Be Made Right.* New York: Waterbrook, 2016.

Hughes, Langston. "Harlem." From *The Collected Works of Langston Hughes.* Copyright © 2002 by Langston Hughes. Reprinted by permission of Harold Ober Associates Inc.

Jacobs, Harriet A. (Linda Brent). *Incidents in the Life of a Slave Girl.* Boston: Self-published, 1861.

Kaba, Mariame. *We Do This 'til We Free Us: Abolitionist Organizing and Transforming Justice.* Chicago: Haymarket, 2021.

Khan-Cullors, Patrisse, and asha bandele. *When They Call You a Terrorist: A Black Lives Matter Memoir.* New York: St. Martin's Griffin, 2017.

King, Martin Luther, Jr. "Conscience and the Vietnam War." In *The Lost Massey Lectures: Recovered Classics from Five Great Thinkers.* Toronto: House of Anansi, 2008.

————. *A Testament of Hope: The Essential Writings and Speeches*, ed. James M. Washington. 1986; repr. New York: HarperCollins, 2003.

————. *The Trumpet of Conscience*. 1967. Repr.: Boston: Beacon Press, 2010.

————. *Why We Can't Wait*, New York: Harper and Row, 1964.

Lorde, Audre. *Sister Outsider*. New York: Ten Speed Press, 1984.

Love, Bettina A. *We Want to Do More Than Survive: Abolitionist Teaching and the Pursuit of Educational Freedom*. Boston: Beacon Press, 2020.

McGuire, Danielle L. *The Dark End of the Street*. New York: Vintage, 2010.

Mitchell, Angelyn, ed. *Within the Circle: An Anthology of African American Literary Criticism from the Harlem Renaissance to the Present*. Durham, NC: Duke University Press, 1994.

Ransby, Barbara. *Ella Baker and the Black Freedom Movement: A Radical Democratic Vision*. Chapel Hill: University of North Carolina Press, 2003.

————. *Making All Black Lives Matter: Reimagining Freedom in the 21st Century*. Oakland: University of California Press, 2008.

Scott, Patricia Bell, Gloria T. Hull, and Barbara Smith, eds. *All the Women Are White, All the Blacks Are Men, But Some of Us Are Brave: Black Women's Studies*. New York: Feminist Press at CUNY, 1982.

Stevenson, Bryan. *Just Mercy: A Story of Justice and Redemption*. New York: Spiegel & Grau, 2014.

Taylor, Keeanga-Yamahtta. *From Black Lives Matter to Black Liberation*. Chicago: Haymarket Books, 2016.

Terry, Brandon, and Tommie Shelby. *To Shape a New World: Essays on the Political Philosophy of Martin Luther King Jr.* Cambridge, MA: Belknap Press of Harvard University Press, 2018.

ARTICLES AND ONLINE POSTINGS

Alexander, Elizabeth. "The Trayvon Generation." *New Yorker*, June 15, 2020.

Brodeur, Michael Andor. "Toni Morrison in Her Own Words: 'The Function of Freedom Is to Free Someone Else.'" *Boston Globe*, August 6, 2019.

Buchanan, Larry. "Black Lives Matter May Be the Largest Movement in U.S. History." *New York Times*, June 6, 2020.

Chuba, Kirsten. "Tarana Burke Says #MeToo Isn't About 'Taking Down Powerful Men'." https://variety.com/video/tarana-burke-metoo-powerful-men/.

Cobb, Jelani. "The Matter of Black Lives." *New Yorker*, March 7, 2016.

Collins, Lauren. "Assa Traoré and the Fight for Black Lives in France." *New Yorker*, June 18, 2020.

Copeland, M. Shawn. "Breath & Fire: The Spirit Moves Us toward Racial Justice." *Commonweal*, July 8, 2020.

Craig, John. "Wesleyan Baccalaureate Is Delivered by Dr. King." *Hartford Courant*, June 8, 1964.

Crawley, Ashon T. "It's Ok to Be Afraid." https://ashoncrawley.com [blog], March 16, 2020.

Crenshaw, Kimberlé. "Demarginalizing the Intersection of Race and Sex: A Black Feminist Critique of Antidiscrimination Doctrine, Feminist Theory and Antiracist Politics." *University of Chicago Legal Forum* 140 (1989): 139–67.

Dahir, Abdi Latif Dahir. "'Instead of Coronavirus, the Hunger Will Kill Us.' A Global Food Crisis Looms." *New York Times*, April 22, 2020.

Delaney, Paul. "Dorothy Height and the Sexism of the Civil Rights Movement." The Root, May 12, 2010, https://www.theroot.com.

Garrow, David J. "The Troubling Legacy of Martin Luther King." Standpoint, June 2019, https://www.davidgarrow.com/wp-content/uploads/2019/05/DJGStandpoint2019.pdf.

Gilmore, Ruth Wilson. "Is Prison Necessary? Ruth Wilson Gilmore Might Change Your Mind." *New York Times Magazine*, April 17, 2019.

———. "Making and Unmaking Mass Incarceration (MUMI)." Keynote conversation between Ruth Wilson Gilmore, Mariame

Kaba, and James Kilgore, MUMI conference, Oxford, Mississippi, December 4, 2019.

Goodrich, Matthew Miles. "The Forgotten Socialist History of Martin Luther King Jr." inthesetimes.com, January 15, 2018.

Grundy, Saida. "The False Promise of Anti-Racism Books." *The Atlantic*, July 21, 2020.

Hooks, Gregory, and Wendy Sawyer. "Mass Incarceration, COVID-19, and Community Spread." Prison Policy Initiative, December 2020, https://www.prisonpolicy.org.

Jackson, Jenn M. "Martin Luther King Jr. Was More Radical Than We Remember: Let's Do His Memory Justice." *Teen Vogue*, May 31, 2010.

Johnson, Christen A. "Black Girls and Women Are Often Left Out of the Social Justice Movement. These 2 Sisters Have Been Fighting to Change That." *Chicago Tribune*, June 19, 2020.

Kaba, Mariame. "Yes, We Literally Mean Abolish the Police." *New York Times*, June 12, 2020.

Kaba, Mariame, and Kelly Hayes. "A Jailbreak of the Imagination: Seeing Prisons for What They Are and Demanding Transformation," Truth Out, May 3, 2018, https://truthout.org.

Killer Mike. "Rapper Killer Mike Speech Transcript during Atlanta Protests." rev.com (blog), May 30, 2020, www.rev.com/blog.

King, Martin Luther, Jr. "Beyond Vietnam." Address delivered at Riverside Church (NYC), April 4, 1967, https://kinginstitute.stanford.edu.

———. "The Christian Way of Life in Human Relations." Address delivered at the General Assembly of the National Council of Churches, St. Louis, Missouri, December 4, 1957, https://kinginstitute.stanford.edu.

———. "A Christmas Sermon on Peace." Sermon delivered at Ebenezer Baptist Church, Atlanta, Georgia, December 24, 1967, https://kinginstitute.stanford.edu.

———. "Conquering Self-Centeredness." Sermon delivered at Dexter Avenue Baptist Church, Montgomery, Alabama, August 11, 1957, http://okra.stanford.edu.

————. "Conscience for Change." CBC Massey Lecture, CBC Radio, November 9, 1967.

————. "The Crisis in America's Cities." Address at the Eleventh Annual Convention of the Southern Christian Leadership Conference, August 15, 1967.

————. "I've Been to the Mountaintop." Speech delivered at the Mason Temple in Memphis, Tennessee, on the day before King was assassinated, April 3, 1968, https://kinginstitute.stanford.edu.

————. "Letter from a Birmingham Jail." April 16, 1963, www.stanford.edu/group/King/popular_requests/frequentdocs/birmingham.pdf.

————. "Loving Your Enemies." Sermon delivered at Dexter Avenue Baptist Church, Montgomery, Alabama, November 17, 1957, http://okra.stanford.edu.

————. "Nonviolence: The Only Road to Freedom." *Ebony*, October 1966, https://teachingamericanhistory.org.

————. "Stride toward Freedom: The Montgomery Bus Boycott." 1957–1958, https://kinginstitute.stanford.edu.

Krischer, Haley. "We're Going to Need More Gabrielle Union." *New York Times*, December 5, 2017.

Ladner, Joyce. "George Floyd's Killing Stirs Old Pain, Anger for a 1960s Activist." *Washington Post*, June 17, 2020.

Lewis, John. "Together, You Can Redeem the Soul of Our Nation." *New York Times*, July 30, 2020.

Lincoln, Abbey. "Who Will Revere the Black Woman?" *Negro Digest,* September 1966. Repr.: ebony.com, February 12, 2013.

Ransby, Barbara. "A Black Feminist's Response to Attacks on Martin Luther King Jr.'s Legacy." *New York Times*, June 3, 2019.

————. "Ella Baker's Legacy Runs Deep, Know Her Name." *New York Times*, January 20, 2020.

Singh, Nikhil Pal. "Reclaiming Populism: From the Dying World to the World We Want." *Boston Review*, April 29, 2020.

Theoharis, Jeanne. "Don't Forget That Martin Luther King Jr. Was Once Denounced as an Extremist." *Time*, January 12, 2018.

Wells, Ida B. "Southern Horrors: Lynch Law in All Its Phases."

1802. Digital History ID 3614, https://www.digitalhistory.uh.edu/disp_textbook_print.cfm?smtid=3&psid=3614.

FILMS

"Fundi": The Story of Ella Baker. Dir. Joanne Grant. Icarus Films, 1981.

Thirteenth. Dir. Ava. DuVernay. Netflix, 2016.

Whose Streets?. Dir. Sabaah Folayan and Damon Davis. Magnolia Pictures, 2017.

Index